THE LOOKOUT

❖

*Society of
Model Shipwrights*

Welcome!

From the archives

Society of Model Shipwrights

The Society will be holding its Biennial Exhibition on Saturday, 23 August 2008 in a new venue, the Petts Wood Memorial Hall, 200 Petts Wood Road, Petts Wood, Kent. Open from 10.00 a.m. to 4.00 p.m. The format will be the same as in the past (but without the Boudriot Prize this year). Entries will be welcome from non-members. Full details of the various competitive classes for ship models, both static and working, maritime vignettes, ships' fittings, and marine paintings may be obtained from the Honorary Secretary, Mr Peter Rogers, 5 Lodge Crescent, Orpington, Kent BR6 0QE.

Welcome!

For the past thirty years we have been without an Assistant Editor. With the changing ship modelling scene and the rapid developments in information technology, I felt that it would be advantageous to have the position filled. Accordingly, I asked that such an appointment be made, and now we are very pleased to welcome aboard Mr Michael Leek MA MPhil(RCA) FRSA in that capacity.

A long-time subscriber to *Model Shipwright*, he has a wide knowledge of ships and ship construction, especially of those during the past two centuries, and of ship modelling. His particular interest lies in late nineteenth-century sail, both commercial and naval, and in local craft types. Information technology advances at a rapid pace; thus his expertise in this field will be of special benefit to the journal, especially later when we will be introducing the *Model Shipwright* web site. In the meantime he will also be involved in furthering some of the suggestions that have surfaced from an assessment of the replies received in the recent questionnaire.

From the archives

Recently a file was found tucked away in the Conway Picture Library that contained a number of images of ship models. The one shown below appears, as indeed do many of the others in the file, to be of a model on show in a London gallery in the early 1960s. Any information on the model and its maker, etc., will be most welcome. ❑

Photograph of a model in a London gallery in the 1960s.

Conway Picture Library

HMS *Alecto* (1882)

by Alan Ludbrook

HMS *Alecto* was described as a special service vessel, designed for anti-slavery patrols and general police work. She was built by Westwood and Baillie at Millwall, London, with engines of 490 ihp made by J & G Rennie, London. Her dimensions were: length bp 160ft 0in, beam 26ft 3in, draught 7ft 4in, displacement 620 tons, complement 68. She was composite built of teak on iron frames, and coppered.

HMS *Alecto* was launched on 14 August 1882, and commissioned at Sheerness on 20 March 1883. She spent all her service life on the West Coast of Africa.

A close sister-ship was HMS *Niger* (renamed *Cockatrice* in 1881), built by John Elder & Co., Govan, Glasgow, in 1880.

Research

Research was fairly easy as highly detailed drawings were available from the National Maritime Museum, Greenwich. The Museum also has two photographs taken at Devonport after her refit in 1891.

The 'As fitted' drawings for the ship show six 25pdr breech loaders mounted on pivoted slides on the upper deck. However, the *Navy Lists* from 1882 to 1891 show her as having only four guns and I presume that two of the midship guns were removed as this part of the ship appears very congested. The drawings also show that two 4-barrelled Gardner machine guns on field mounts were carried on the Hurricane deck. These could be wheeled to various fighting positions round the deck.

The model

This is a radio-controlled working model, built to a scale of 1:48 (¼in = 1ft), and represents HMS *Alecto* as built. The hull was constructed on the plank-on-frame method, using

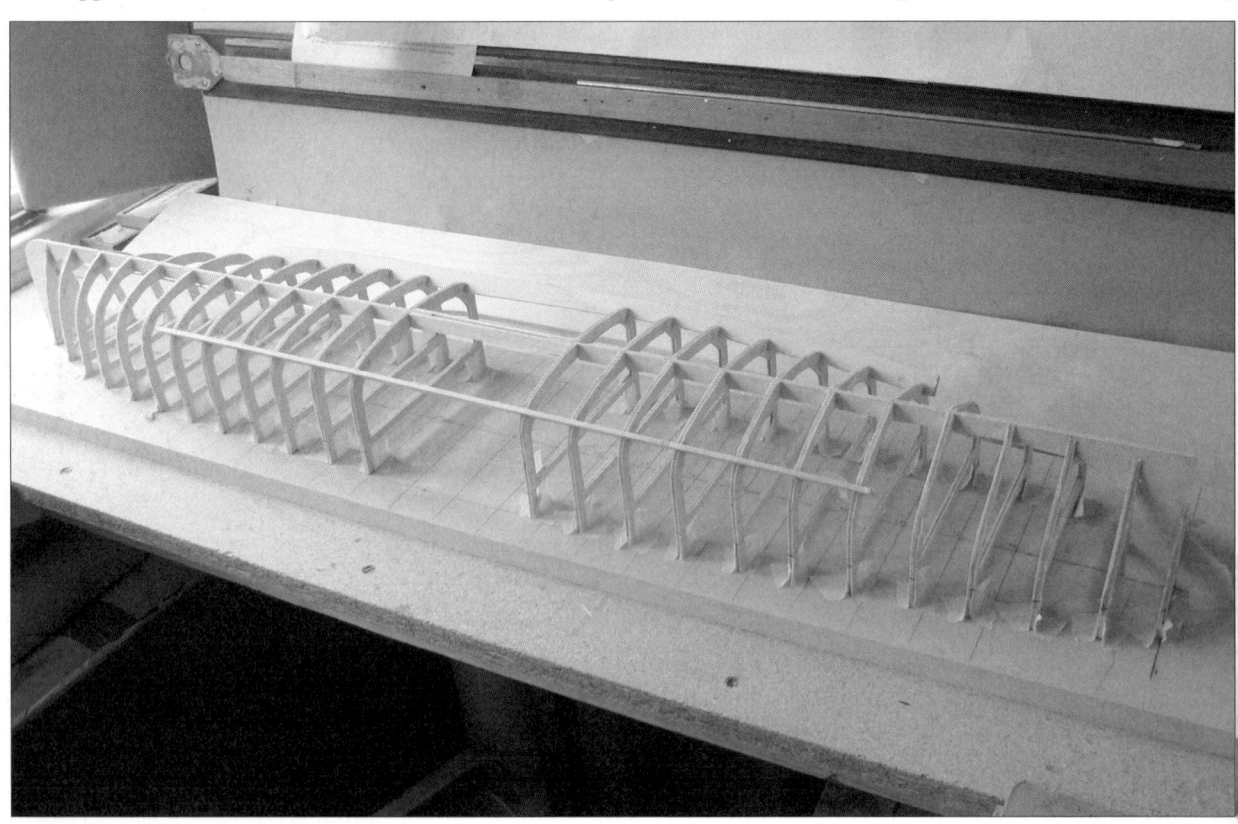

Model in frame. Note bilge keels let into frames.

Model planked.

Upper deck prior to fitting the Hurricane Deck.

Upper deck forward.

Lathe and Carpenter's bench.

⅛in marine plywood for the keel and frames. On the original ship the bilge keels were 85ft long and 12in deep. To provide additional longitudinal strength on the model the bilge keels, normally attached externally to the hull, were inserted into slots cut in the frames before fitting the hull planking. These keels were made of ⅛in marine plywood ½in wide, of which ¼in projected outside the hull planking. Fitting these keels in this way allowed some frames to be omitted amidships where the hull is parallel-sided, thereby providing more room for fitting the drive mechanism. On the model two through beams of 6mm square hardwood were fitted forward and aft of the paddle wheels. These formed the main support for the sponsons, which were securely attached to the hull. The hull was planked with strips of marine ply, ¼in wide by ¹⁄₁₆in thick. The edges of each plank above the waterline were slightly cham-

fered, to form a narrow groove with its neighbours, which remained visible after painting, thus indicating the hull planking. When the planking had been completed, the interior was coated with resin. Below the waterline *Alecto*'s hull was copper plated. On the model this was done by gluing pieces of thin card cut to represent the 4ft long by 15in wide copper plates. A contemporary drawing showed that the bilge keels were coppered. The heads of the nails, which secured the plates to the hull on the original ship, were reproduced by running a pounce wheel along and close to the edges of the cards. This produced a row of 'pimples' on the other side of the card.

The removable upper deck was laminated from three sheets of ½in plywood to form an under deck. This was taped to the hull to dry, so that it would conform to the sheer of the hull. When quite set it was then planked with strips of 1mm thick

lime of appropriate width. The Hurricane Deck was formed from a single sheet of ½in plywood. This was planked with strips of 1mm thick lime, with beams fitted on the underside. The boiler casing, etc., were made of thin plywood and plated with card.

Boats

From the drawings it was apparent that frequent changes were made to the outfit of boats carried. The original one appeared to have been: one 25ft steam cutter, two 25ft whalers, one 25ft whale or surf boat, one 24ft gig, one 14ft dinghy. For the model the boats were based on the superb resin boats obtained from Quaycraft but modified to represent the above types. The whalers were made from the Quaycraft 27ft whaler with a ½in section removed amidships. The steam cutter was made from a ship's clinker lifeboat, but the hull was covered with filler and sanded to repre-

Stern gun platform.

Wardroom and Captain's cabin.

sent a carvel hull. A drawing of a 25ft steam cutter of 1888 obtained from the National Maritime Museum provided the information for the deck layout and internal fittings. All the boats except the dinghy were carried on the Hurricane Deck, and were handled by radial davits. These were made from tapered brass rod.

Paddle wheels

The paddle wheels are fully feathering. They were made from brass blanks, which are available from Waverley Models. Though designed for a scale model of the still operating well-known paddle steamer *Waverley*, they were just the right diameter, although the hub had to be modified to conform to the scale width. New floats had to be made, for which marine plywood was used.

Because the paddle shaft cannot pass through the feathering mechanism on the outside of the paddle

wheels it had to be made in two pieces with a sleeve joint. This allowed the shafts to be withdrawn from the inside of the hull.

Power plant and E/C gear

A 12-volt motor with an integral gearbox was used to drive the paddle wheels. The motor had a circular casing with no mounting flanges. As the motor drove the paddle shaft via gears, considerable torque was developed, and it was essential that the motor was secure. Eventually a sturdy beam was fitted under the motor and the latter were screwed to the beam with two screwed metal hose clips. Both wheels are on the driven shaft. This geared-down motor drives the paddle wheels at 60 rpm. Originally the motor was to have been connected to two 6-volt sealed gel batteries in series. However, they proved to be too bulky. At present they have been replaced by

two battery boxes each containing four type D cells. These are fitted in the hull just forward and aft of the boxes enclosing the companionways down from the upper deck.

The radio control installation is a simple two-channel unit. The power on/off switch is operated, when the deck is fitted, by poking a rod down the forward funnel.

Access to the interior of the hull is always a problem in a model of a paddle steamer, so in this case the whole upper deck, with the superstructure, was made removable. When removed, the deck stands on the two boxes constructed to house the companionways down from the upper deck.

The bow rudder is non operable, and a dummy tiller for the stern rudder is fitted under the raised gun platform at the stern. This allows the tiller ropes for both rudders to be permanently fitted.

After boiler casing.

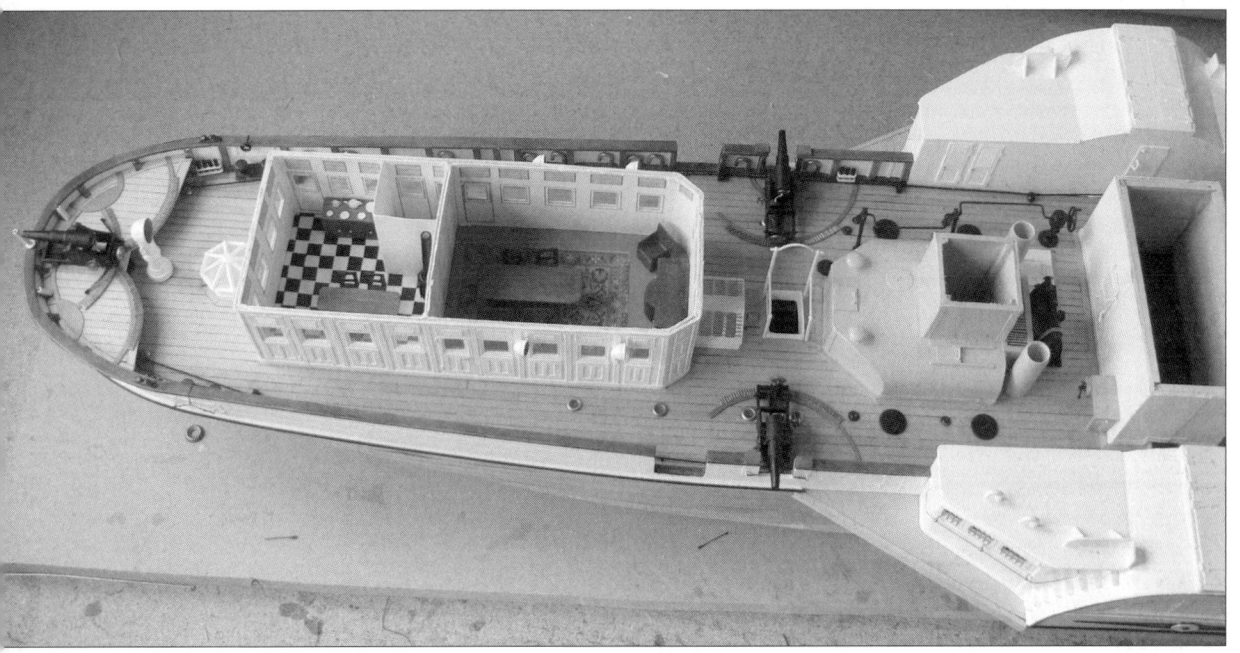

Upper deck aft.

Armament

The 25pdr gun barrels were made from assembling gradually shorter lengths of increasing diameter brass tube to obtain a roughly tapered shape. This was then spun in an electric drill mounted on the bench and smoothed with a file. The gun carriage and slides were made from various plastic sections available from model shops. There are shell racks round the bulwarks and the drawings clearly show the shells with their pointed end facing downwards. The Gardener machine gun barrels were made from four lengths of very fine brass tube mounted in a block, which, on the original, would have contained the rapid fire breech arrangement operated by turning a handle at the side. The magazines were mounted vertically over the breech block and the magazine chutes were represented with some very fine brass channel. The wheels for the field carriages were rather fiddly to make, and were made on a simple jig. I drew out the wheels and spokes were drawn on a piece of wood. This was then drilled to take a dummy axle. Locating pins were inserted between the spoke positions to centre the rim accurately on the axle. The wheel hub was then placed on the dummy axle and the wheel rim, made from a slice of plastic tube, placed between the locating pins. At each spoke position a hole was drilled through the rim and then just slightly into the hub. Spokes of brass wire were inserted through the rim with the ends located in the hub. All the joints were dabbed with superglue, being careful not to glue the wheel to the jig. When dry the wheel was removed, the protruding end of each spoke snipped off flush with the rim, and a tyre of black card glued to the circumference of the wheel. The elevating, traversing and brake hand wheels for all the guns were from etched brass sheet obtained from Scale Link.

The tracks of the gun races were difficult to make and in the end, after trying various methods, the races were made out of flat material, with short lengths of rod glued on to represent the teeth.

Miscellaneous fittings

The cowl ventilators were made from plastic tube with moulded plastic cowls or commercial items if suitable. All ventilators were fitted with turning handles. There are also twenty-

Cook's table.

Forge.

First tests afloat.

Hull and removable upper deck.

eight gooseneck ventilators located round the edge of the upper deck. These were made from brass wire.

The anchors were all of Admiralty pattern. Two 15 cwt anchors forward were carried on anchor tables with quick release gear. The anchor cables passed through chain stoppers. A 7 cwt anchor with its stock stowed was located on each quarter. The anchors were carved from wood and the stocks made from brass wire.

According to the drawings, neither a windlass nor cable lifters were fitted. A capstan was fitted forward, and this was made by assembling discs and tubes of different diameter on a central core, with the whelps added afterwards. The base of the capstan was fitted with guide rollers.

The stanchions for the guard rails were purchased. The supports for the screens round the companionways and the awning stanchions

Starboard quarter view.

Broadside view.

were made from brass wire and rod.

All the cabins were panelled in thin card. The louvres above the windows were made from plastic 'corrugated iron' sheets, available from model railway suppliers.

The upper deck cabins were furnished (the Captain's Cabin has a carpet cut from an illustration in a catalogue), and in the midship area between the paddle boxes a treadle lathe, forge, carpenter's bench and the cook's table have been fitted, but unfortunately, little of this detail is visible when the Hurricane Deck has been fitted. Stowage racks for boarding pike were fitted on the forward cabin. The bevel gear drives for the engine room telegraphs were fitted on the underside of the Hurricane Deck before it was finally installed.

She carried a simple schooner rig and could set a square sail flying on the foremast.

The hull and upperworks were painted white with some black detailing. The funnels, boiler casing and some of the larger cowl ventila-

Starboard bow view.

Boarding pike racks on fore side of cabin. Bevel gear drives for Engine Room telegraphs under Hurricane Deck.

tors were painted buff.

With her simple rig and light coloured livery she was a handsome ship.

The displacement of the model in full working order is 12.5lb (about 5.68kg). There is a ballast weight of about 1lb, which had to be carefully positioned to compensate for the unavoidable off-centre positioning of the motor. When underway she is rather tender and not really suitable for rough weather conditions. The rudder fitted was to scale size, and produced a large turning circle.

She was a handsome little vessel and may be the only late-Victorian

One of the fully feathering paddle wheels.

Overhead starboard quarter view.

Paddle wheel drive.

warship whose commander was killed in action.

References

The Royal Navy by William Laird Clowes and the official *Navy Lists* for the ship's history.

Suppliers

Waverley Models, 20B Moor Lane, Clevedon, Somerset BS21 6ES

Quaycraft, 73 Chambercomb Road, Ilfracombe, North Devon

Scale Link, Farrington, Dorset DT11 8RA

James Lane (Display Models), 30 Broadway, Blyth, Northumberland NE24 2PP

History

In 1891 she was recalled to Devonport for a refit. The 25pdr guns were

Ship's boats.

replaced with two 4-inch guns placed just forward of the paddle sponsons, and she was provided with a battery of Gardner and Nordenfeldt machine guns on permanent mounts. Other changes made at this time were the removal of the bow rudder and improvements to the ventilation. She was re-commissioned at Devonport on 28 October 1891.

HMS *Alecto* spent all her service life on the West Coast of Africa. Apart from anti-slavery patrols the *Alecto* was frequently in action, mostly in joint Army and Navy expeditions, several of which were part of the notorious 'Scramble for Africa' of the late nineteenth century.

In October 1883 she took part in actions at both Igah and Aboh on the River Niger, and then in December 1886 she was in action at Patani on the same river following the pillaging of a Niger Company factory.

In the spring of 1891 she took part in the Campaign against Chief Fodeh Cabbah who had attacked an Anglo-French boundary commission in the Gambia, while the following year she took part in the expedition against Chief Carimoo who had established a stronghold at Tambi on the River Scarcies, raided natives under British protection and attacked the Sierra Leone police force.

In early 1894 she took part in the expedition against Chief Fodeh Sillah on the Gambia. In August of that year her captain, Lieutenant John George Heugh took the steam cutter to investigate some trouble on the Benin River. They were fired on by a masked battery ashore and several men were killed and wounded. They managed to fire a rocket into the battery and then the cutter, steered by Heugh and driven by a wounded stoker, steamed back to the *Alecto* in a sinking condition and with its gun dismounted. Lieutenant Heugh was awarded the DSO and Chief Gunners Mate H Crouch was awarded the Conspicuous Gallantry Medal. As a result of this engagement, a major punitive expedition was mounted against Chief Nanna.

In February 1897 she participated in the Benin campaign where her captain, Lt Charles Edward Pritchard, was killed in action. In 1898 she took an active part in the Sierra Leone Hut Tax War, after which she was sold out of service in Sierra Leone on 12 October 1899. ❑

Showing sundry deck fittings.

Photographs by the author.

Marine Paintings and Ship Models

❧

by Michael Pope (SMS)

I have been making ship models over a period of more than fifty years (on and off) and have derived a huge amount of enjoyment and satisfaction from doing so. In the same period I have also tried to progress my interest in marine paintings. Thus when the Editor recently asked if I had 'any articles in the offing', I said I had no new model to write about, but would be happy to write something about my paintings. He agreed that I should do this, hence this article.

I am proposing to comment on the various paintings (and the ships they show) which illustrate the article, and mention connections with my models where these exist. I am dividing the article into four groups, namely:

• fast sailing monohulls
• *La Salamandre*
• square-rigged ships
• various others

But before reaching this stage, I would like to offer some general thoughts on paintings and models. The first point to make is that both disciplines seek to provide the viewer with a representation of a vessel, and thus both require a degree of research to enable this representation to be accurate. Paintings almost invariably show a vessel as part of a wider scene, while models may attempt the same where the vessel is set in the water, often in the form of a diorama. On the other hand, probably more models make no such attempt, being displayed on a stand, and hopefully in a case. I do not think it is possible to say that a model is preferable to a painting or vice versa, although what is generally true is that models require a much greater expenditure of time than paintings.

In my own case, my basic approach is more of a modeller than a painter. This means that I concentrate on accuracy of representation of the vessel in my paintings, but also tend to allow my paintings to become more finicky than is desirable. I have to struggle to avoid using fine brushes more than necessary.

I use both water colours and oils, although recently have concentrated on the latter. One of the problems with oils is that they require a lengthy drying time, and in order to overcome this I have taken to using Winsor and Newton Griffin Alkyd fast drying Titanium White. This I use in conjunction with ordinary colour oils, and find that a day's work will usually dry overnight. I also ensure that I use best quality paints – whether oil or water colour.

The major areas in a marine painting are usually taken up by the sky and sea, so one has to develop techniques to represent these. I try to ensure that the sky does not dominate the picture, using thin coats of paint, whereas I use much thicker paint for the sea. One of the fascinating aspects of marine art is the very wide range of techniques for painting seas used by the leading artists: some adopt an almost photographic approach, while others use their paint very loosely. I try to fall between the two extremes, aiming to give the impression of movement.

It is also important to ensure that the wind direction and strength are indicated accurately: by the set of the sails, the amount of sail carried, the flags, the movement of the sea and of the clouds. I leave it to others to decide how well I have succeeded as I move on to describe the paintings that illustrate this article.

Medium used and approximate sizes are given for the images (height x width in inches): where these are followed by 'D', the image shown is a detail of the larger whole.

Fast sailing monohulls

1. HM Cutter *Speedy* (1828)
Water colour, 9in x 12in, and oil on canvas, 11in x 16in

Cutters have always been one of my favourite types of vessel. They carried huge spreads of sail and were regarded as the fastest sailing vessels in the latter part of the eighteenth century. They were thus invaluable for carrying dispatches and chasing smugglers. *Speedy* therefore is an appropriate vessel to start this group. Her main dimensions were nearly 65ft length on deck, 22ft breadth, but nearly 120ft overall length when rigged.

I made a model of *Speedy* at 1:64 scale some twenty-eight years ago. An article about this model appeared in *MS100*, and Photograph A gives a view of it.

Over the years I have painted a number of pictures of her, made easier by having the model for reference. I show two of these here: the first is a water colour in a calm sea (Photograph B), and the second an oil in a fresh breeze (Photograph C). The latter illustrates the huge area of canvas carried by the cutters, even though she carries no drabblers,

A. Author's model of HMS *Speedy*.

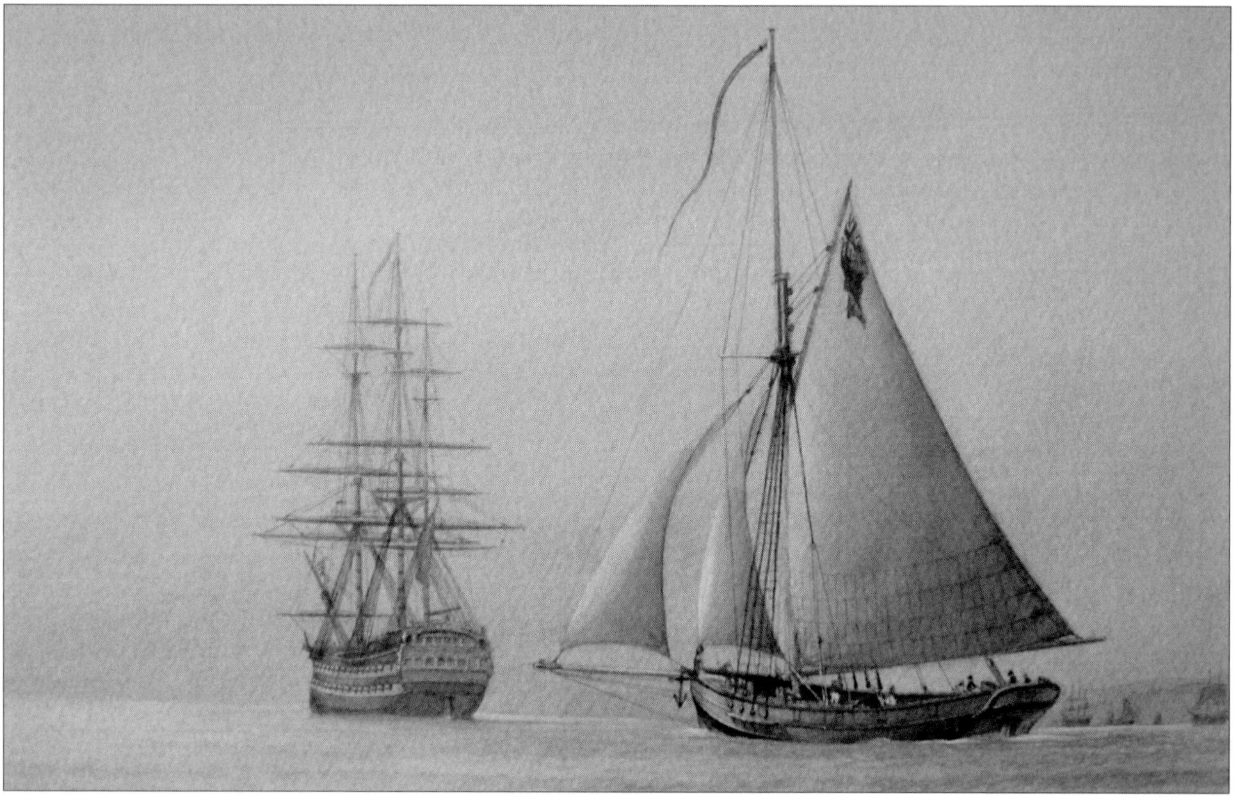

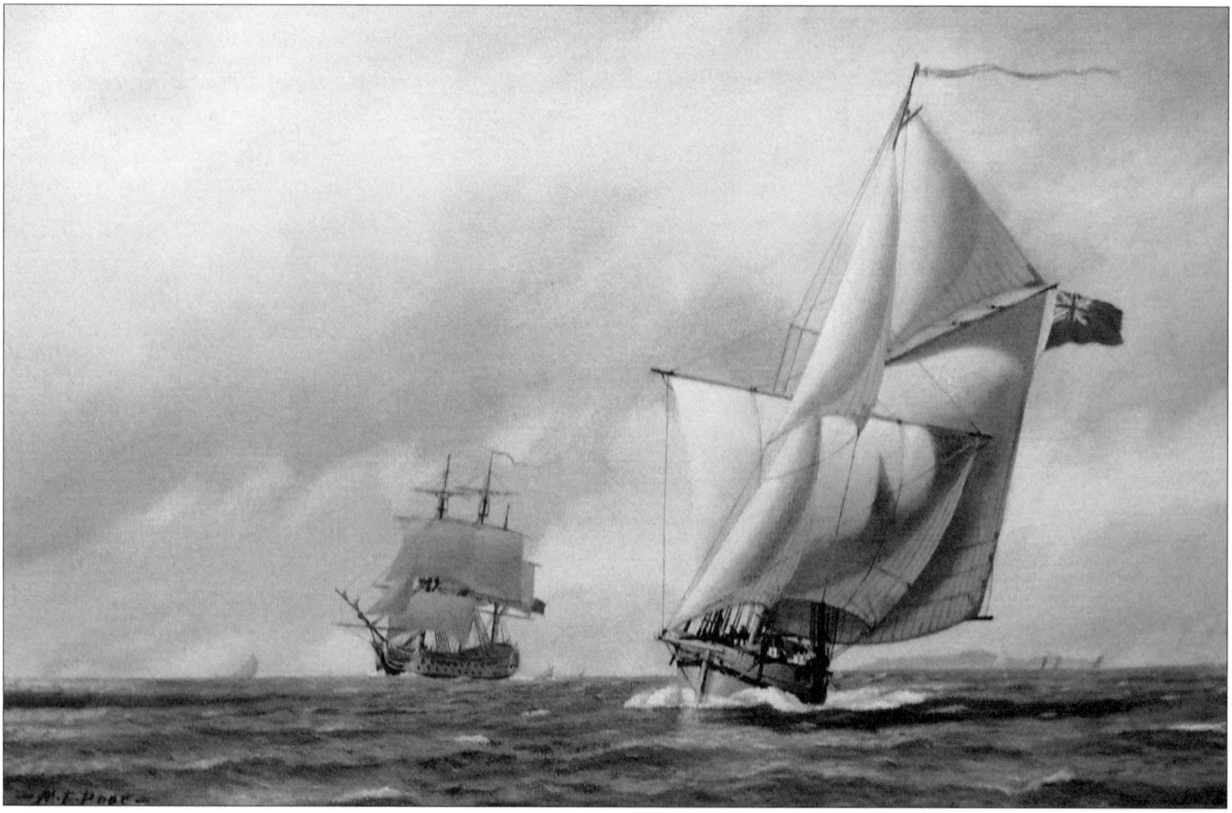

B. & C. HMS *Speedy*.

ringtails, water sails, running mizzen or other exotica.

2. *Shamrock* 23-metre (1908)
Oil on canvas board, 18in x 24in

The sport of yachting first came to prominence in the early part of the nineteenth century. To start with, yachts were built on very similar lines to cutters, but towards the end of the century hull shapes changed to give spoon bows and long counters. The wealthiest owners sailed in the 'big class', of which *Britannia*, built in 1893, was undoubtedly the best known. A typical example is *Shamrock*, built in 1908 to the 23-metre rule by Fife (of Fairlie, Ayrshire, Scotland) for Sir Thomas Lipton. She is not to be confused with the five

Shamrocks which Lipton had built in order to challenge for the America's Cup, all of which were unsuccessful. The 23-metre, however, had a very successful career, and continued to race until the early 1930s when the J class rule was adopted for the big class.

When built she carried a rig which was similar in principle to that of a cutter, but in the 1920s the fidded mainmast and topmast were replaced by a single spar, nicknamed a Marconi rig. However, the similarity in rig to that of *Speedy* is still noticeable, albeit that a spinnaker replaced the square running sails. The painting (Photograph D) shows her running past East Cowes and carrying her enormous spinnaker, which increased the overall sail area from about 9,000 sq ft to 17,000 sq

ft. The sun is shining on the pristine canvas, a fresh squall has kicked up white horses, and the yacht travels at near her maximum speed.

For a long time after the Second World War it was thought that such big class yachts would never be seen again. However, there are now three J class yachts restored and in commission – *Endeavour*, *Shamrock V* and *Velsheda* – together with a replica of *Ranger*, the last American J Class. The most recent news is that a replica of Sopwith's second *Endeavour* is under construction and due to be launched in 2009.

There are also four 23-metre yachts in commission, *Candida*, *Astra*, *Cambria*, and most recently *Lulworth*. The latter carries a gaff rig, while the other three have Bermudan rigs.

D. *Shamrock*.

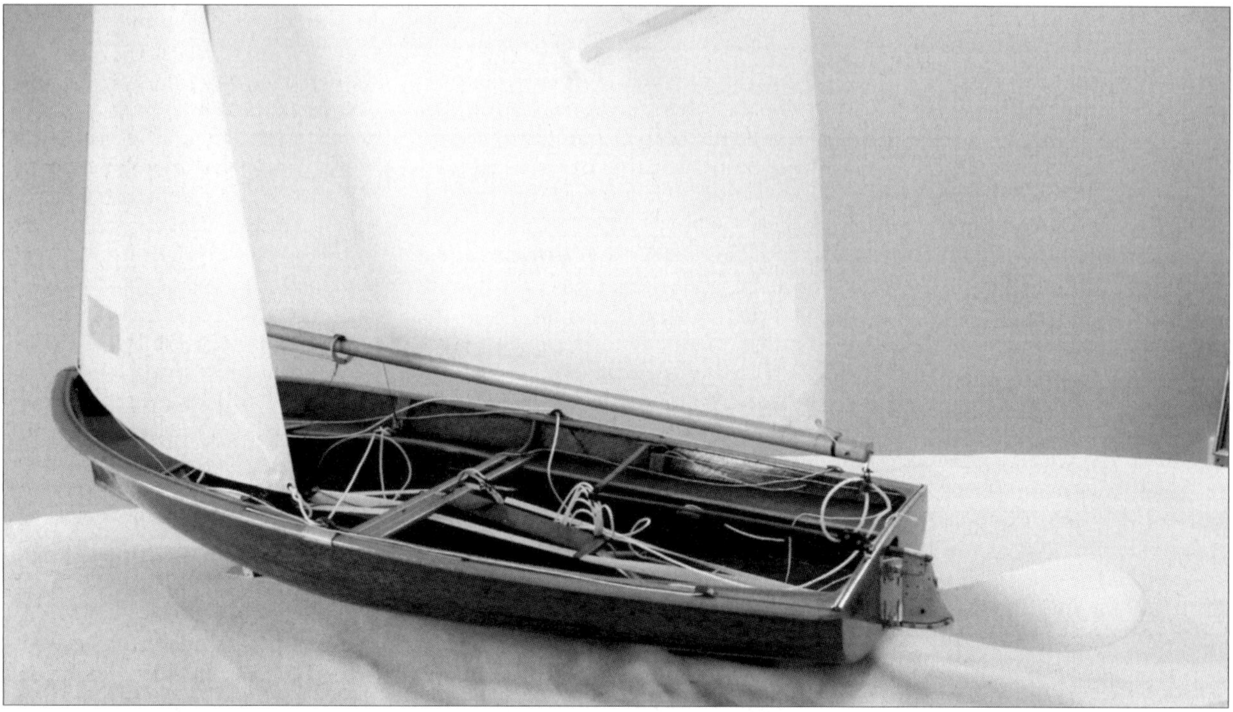

E. Author's model of *Bolero*.

3. *Bolero*, International 14ft Class (1956)

Oil on board, 15in x 28in, D

In the 1920s a racing class was developed for 14ft dinghies, firstly a national class and then international. Initially these were heavy clinker boats, but they soon developed into much lighter craft, with flat runs and sharp bows. This enabled them to plane over the water when off the wind, and thus sailed much faster than the old heavy displacement boats. This trend was largely down to Uffa Fox, who was without doubt the leading designer and builder of fourteens throughout the 1930s.

His boats were beautifully built, and about twenty-five years ago I built a model of Uffa's 1935 dinghy *Alarm* at 1½in = 1ft scale. An article about *Alarm* appeared in *MS50*, and since then the model has been on display at the National Maritime Museum Cornwall. The article also referred to *Bolero*, a later dinghy

F. *Bolero*.

G. *ABN AMRO One.*

designed and built by Austin Farrer in 1956. I sailed as crew in *Bolero* in the late 1950s, and made a model of her in 1960. I show here a picture of this model (Photograph E), and also a painting (Photograph F).

The painting shows *Bolero* leading the fleet on the Friday of the 1956 Prince of Wales Cup week in Torbay. She carries a huge red spinnaker made by Herbulot of Paris, who was then the 'in' person for such sails. We won that race by a comfortable margin, some compensation for a dismal showing in the main race on the previous day when an almost total lack of wind turned the race into a lottery.

Although these dinghies are not visually very appealing, with their vertical stems and sterns, they are nevertheless very exciting to sail in fresh conditions and I hope the picture gives an indication of this.

As a postscript, since the *Bolero* era, the class has changed out of all recognition. Fibreglass or carbon fibre have replaced wood in the hull construction, and the boats have trapezes for helmsman and crew, with big masthead asymmetrical spinnakers set on retractable bowsprits.

4. *ABN AMRO One,* Volvo Open 70, 2005

Oil on canvas board, 18in x 22in
For a long time it was thought to be impossible for the planing type of yacht design to be used for boats larger than dinghies, because the power/weight ratio could only be achieved by using the weight of the crew to keep the boat upright. However, recent technical developments have shown this to be untrue.

A good illustration of the modern ocean racer is the class used in the 2005/2006 Volvo round-the-world ocean race, of which *ABN AMRO One* is the prime example, having won the race overall by a substantial margin. The hull shape is very similar to that of a racing dinghy, but at 70ft is very much larger. Much of the construction is of carbon fibre, and a very deep and narrow keel with a heavy bulb is incorporated with a canting mechanism. This enables the keel to be raised on the windward side to give increased stability. The rig is tall, with a wide variety of headsails.

Their appearance is a world away from the classic boats of the twentieth century. *ABN* has a hull which is basically black (which gave rise to her nickname of Black Betty), but this carries a sweep of yellow from the bow aft, which meets a sweep of blue amidships. The mainsail is also multi-coloured, and

H. *La Salamandre.*

headsails vary from gold to white. The boat has its name and other wording written in many places on the hull and rig. Altogether, this is a most colourful sight, although the amount of sign writing in the picture requires new skills to be learnt by the artist!

My painting (Photograph G) shows the yacht in the North Atlantic, flying down the face of a big wave. The crew crouch in discomfort as the spray washes over them. Life on board is unimaginable: cold, wet, exhausting, terrifying at times and exhilarating at others. The speed of these boats is extraordinary: the record for distance covered in twenty-four hours by a monohull yacht was increased to over 560 nautical miles during this race. An average speed of well over 20 knots means that top speeds must reach around 40 knots!

La Salamandre

Three images, each ink and water colour, 13in x 10in, D

La Salamandre was a French bomb ketch of 1752, and has become well known since M Jean Boudriot and Hubert Berti wrote a monograph about her in 1982. The monograph included the most complete set of drawings that a modeller could desire, and in 1983 I began a 1:48 scale model of her. This was not completed until 2001: I wrote an article about her construction, which appeared in *MS121*.

La Salamandre was 86ft in length, and carried two forward facing mortars in the forward half of the hull, with eight 6pdr long guns in the after half. The mainmast was very tall, and placed about amidships, with a small mizzen and no foremast.

Having spent eighteen years working on the model, I had become very familiar with the detail of the vessel. So when I was asked to paint a picture to form the dust jacket of the English version of the monograph, I was very happy to accept.

Composing a single picture, which would wrap around the front, back and spine of the book, as well as fitting in with the wording, presented an interesting challenge. My first attempt, done in ink and water colour, showed two views of the vessel close hauled in a fresh breeze, the larger image for the back and a smaller one for the front. Photograph I shows the front cover view.

J. BOUDRIOT – H. BERTI

Translated by DAVID H. ROBERTS

THE BOMB KETCH

SALAMANDRE
1752

COLLECTION ARCHÉOLOGIE NAVALE FRANÇAISE

I. & J. Paintings for dust jacket of the English edition of *La Salamandre* book.

However, when at sea, the mortars were covered by a rope and tarpaulin deck, and the authors felt that the cover illustration should show the operation of the mortars, so I did a totally new painting, also in ink and water colour. This showed three separate images of the vessel, following a common convention of nineteenth-century marine art. For the front cover I showed a view of the ketch approaching the shore, and getting ready to anchor so as to be able to start bombarding the enemy. Photograph J shows the front cover as published. On the back part of the cover I showed the vessel moored, with the mortars being set up. Photograph K shows this back cover view. The cable mainstay has been taken down and replaced with that made of chain, and the rest of the fore rigging has been removed to avoid the risk of

fire. In the distant background is the third image.

Fortunately this painting was accepted by the authors, and was published as shown.

Square-rigged ships

1. English ships at sea, 1673
Oil on canvas, 28in x 36in
This picture was inspired by a small sketch made by van der Velde the Elder. The two major ships were identified by Frank Fox in his *Great Ships* as being, on the right, the two-decker *Victory*, and in the centre the three-decker *Charles*.

Victory was originally built at Deptford as a 60-gun ship, but very substantially rebuilt in 1666 to become an 80-gun vessel. The *Charles* was a 96-gun ship built at Deptford and launched in 1668. She was the first great ship to be built by Charles II following his restoration.

In the left foreground is a pink, a small Dutch fishing boat.

To provide the detail of the larger ships there are three portrait drawings by the Elder of *Charles* and one of *Victory*. One feature of the three-decker was that a gallery was constructed across the break of the forecastle, which was apparently unique. This can be seen in the painting (Photograph L).

2. French 74-gun ship
Water colour, 8in x 12in
This water colour shows a French 74 (Photograph M), based on M Jean Boudriot's great four-volume work entitled the *74-gun Ship*. I have copies of both the original French version and the later English version. These have provided enormous pleasure as well as instruction: in my view they are unmatched both for the text, the plans and the amazing drawings.

K. Painting for dust jacket of the English edition of *La Salamandre* book.

3. *Victory*, 1805

Oil on board, 24in x 36in, D

Nearly every marine artist has at some time painted Nelson's *Victory*, and this is my attempt (Photograph N). I do not think any further comment is needed.

4. *Ariel*, 1866

Oil on canvas, 20in x 30in

The same comment applies to this clipper ship as to the *Victory*. So much has been written and published about the famous tea races and in particular, the race between *Ariel*, *Taeping* and *Serica*. However, I do find that in spite of the huge number of paintings of this subject, it is rare to find an artist who can successfully convey the true shape of these vessels. One of the problems is that the sides of the hull are long and largely without detail – unlike the sailing warship.

My painting (Photograph O) shows *Ariel* in the 1866 Tea Race, probably the most famous of these races. She is sailing into the English Channel, with the Devon coast just in sight on her port side. She carries all possible canvas. Astern *Taeping* can be seen in the distance, while out of sight in the Southern Channel *Serica* is also well in the race. The three had left the Min River in China on the same tide, and after nine days of racing, all arrived in the Channel at the same time.

These three ships all docked in London on the same tide. There was some argument as to who really won the race, and the captains were afraid that in the event of a dispute, the merchants might try to avoid paying the winner's premium. They accordingly made a private agreement that *Taeping* should be regarded as the winner, and they would split the premium between them.

5. *Georg Stage*, 1998

Oil on board, 24in x 36in

In 1998 the Tall Ships week took place in Falmouth. On the Thursday I was lucky enough to secure a place on board *Eve*. She is a replica pilot cutter, built by Luke Powell, which operates out of St Mawes, taking people for day or longer trips.

On the day in question there was a good fresh breeze, and, with a couple of reefs in the mainsail, we sailed out into the bay. Before long we saw a three-masted ship on the horizon, and soon after she tacked to make her way into the harbour. We came up to her and followed her in, having seen that she was the Danish training ship *Georg Stage*. I took many photographs of her, and later decided the scene would make an impressive painting. Photograph P shows the result.

In the picture, St Anthony's Head lighthouse can be seen between the vessels, and St Mawes Castle in the distance beyond *Georg Stage*.

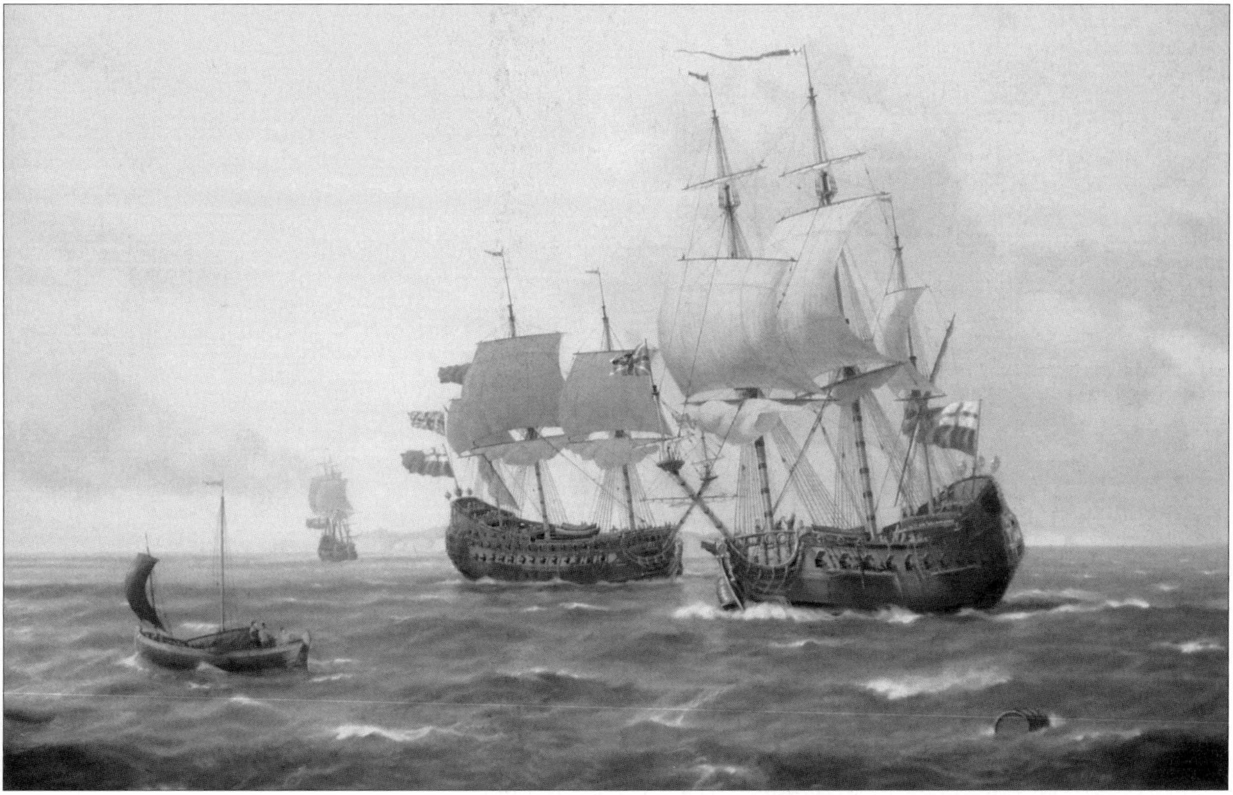

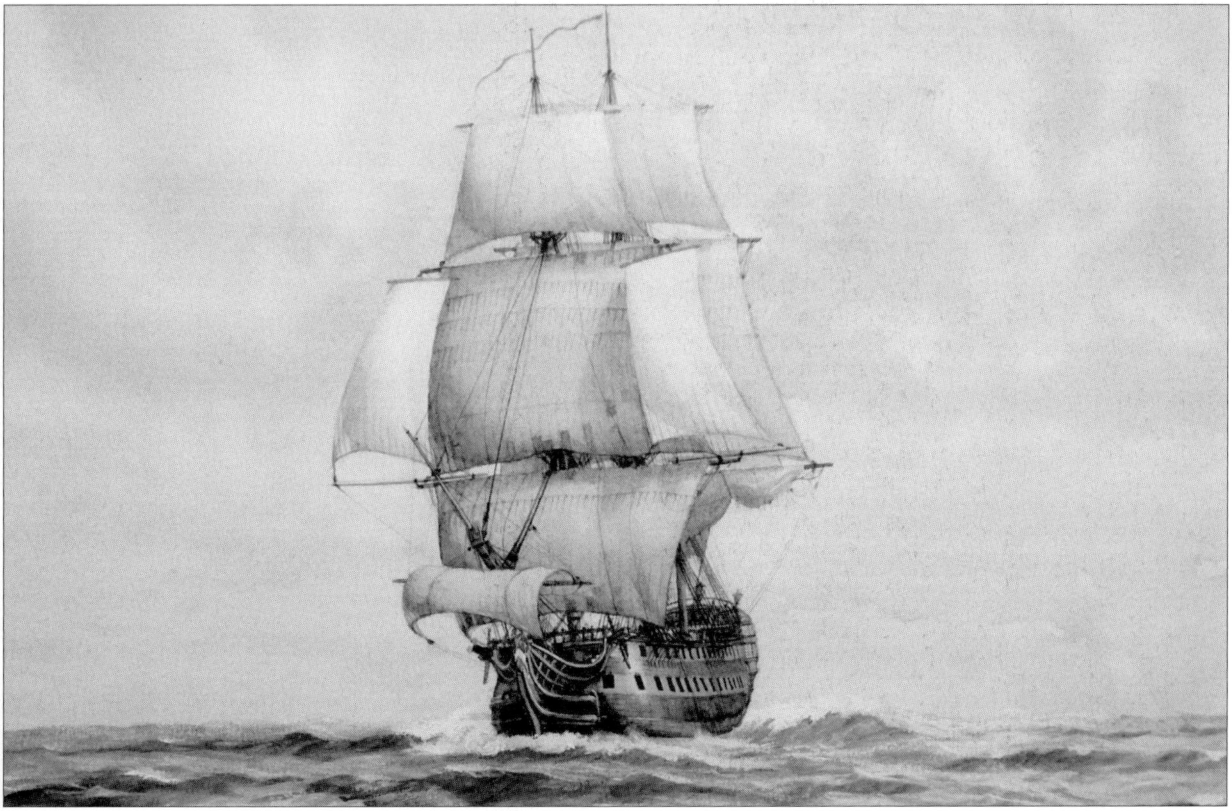

N. HMS *Victory*.

Other Paintings

1. *Lady Cristal*, 2007

Oil on board, 12in x 23in

This is rather different in that the major vessel, a 70ft motor yacht, has no sails! The portrait of *Lady Cristal* was done for her owner, who lives in Tampa, Florida. Having never seen the vessel, I had to rely on the photographs he was able to provide, which proved to be more than adequate.

The painting is in oils on board: the shape of the board was chosen to reflect the comparatively long and low vessel. To avoid a painting without any sail on view, I introduced a few yachts – they also provided colour. Fortunately, the owner seems to be delighted with the picture (Photograph Q).

2. HM Submarine *A1*

Water colour, 10in x 14in

To recognise the centenary of the introduction of the submarine into the Royal Navy, the Society of Model Shipwrights adopted the theme of submarines for its 2002 biennial exhibition. I did not feel able to make a model, but as the Society also welcomes paintings, I decided to show a water colour of a submarine.

I found sufficient literature to provide the information I needed, and chose HM Submarine *A1* as my subject. The first class of submarine to be acquired by the navy was the Holland, of which five were built. The 'A' class followed in about 1905.

The painting shows the submarine with HMS *Dreadnought* in the background (Photograph R). There is also a Thames barge in the dis-

tance to ensure some sail appears in the picture.

3. *Hastings Beach*, c.1900

Ink and water colour, 14in x 22in

One of the few places where wooden working boats can still be seen operating from the beach is at Hastings, Sussex. Although they are of course now powered by engines, the basic boats have changed little for many years. I have visited the beach a number of times, and painted many of the boats there.

For my painting, I have gone back to the 1900 era (Photograph S). The strange object in the left foreground is a horse winch, which was used to pull the boats out of the water and up the beach.

The Hastings Old Town Museum has much of interest in the way of the local fishing industry and craft. ❏

O. Tea clipper *Ariel*.

P. *Georg Stage.*

Q. *Lady Cristal.*

R. HM Submarine *A1*.

S. Hastings (Sussex) beach, *c.*1900.

Photographs by the author.

Jervis Bay

by Mark Slota

One of the great David and Goliath sea engagements of the Second World War was the one-sided duel between HMS *Jervis Bay* and the German pocket battleship *Admiral Scheer* during November 1940. *Jervis Bay* was built in 1922 by Vickers Ltd, Barrow-in-Furness, for the Australian Government as a passenger-emigrant cargo carrier. Displacement was 23,230 tons and length 549ft overall.

In August 1939 she was taken over and fitted out as an armed merchant cruiser, fitted with eight 6in guns, and repainted Admiralty-grey, becoming HMS *Jervis Bay*. Early in November 1940 she escorted convoy HX 84 comprising thirty-eight ships, with a speed about half that of the *Scheer*. For two hours she drew the fire from the German ship, allowing the convoy to escape via a smoke screen. Only six ships were lost in total, and surprisingly *Scheer* was not used again effectively. Commander of *Jervis Bay*, Captain E S Fogarty was awarded a posthumous Victoria Cross (the only one for convoy defence).

My choice of subject was the result of the recent publication *If the Gods are Good* by G Duskin & R Segman, which describes the event and includes some useful illustrations. In addition I obtained from the National Maritime Museum, Greenwich, a photograph of the 1:48 scale model, which is in the Aberdeen Line's dark green hull colour.

The model

For the model I used the plan of the sister-ship *Esperance Bay*, No. 11 in the series of 'Historic Liners' by R Carpenter, published in the May 1961 issue of *Modelmaker*. The model was built to a scale of 50ft = 1in (1/600), giving a hull length of about 11in (28cm) overall.

The hull is carved from pearwood and faced with 0.010in Plasticard, which extends to the bulwarks; the portholes were drilled prior to fitting in place. I did the artwork for decks to a large scale then used a laser colour copier to reduce it to the scale size. The colour and shade can also be varied by trial and error; some will be kept for future projects. The deckhouses were built up using plastic square sections and plastic sheet, which is relatively easy to finish. Masts and derricks were shaped from brass rod, painted buff. A piece of plastic tube was used to make the funnel. The lifeboats were moulded in plastic on a wooden former. Fly-tying thread, as used in fishing and conveniently black, was used for the rigging. I find a prelimi-

The model ready for the case and simulated sea.

Port side showing a little weathering.

Aft end. Extensions below waterline are blobs of car repair resin blended into the hull by sanding.

Fore end. Stanchions are copper wire built in a frame together with rails.

nary study of photographs of ships at sea invaluable in determining a suitable sea setting for a model. After trying out several different methods for making a sea my favoured one is to use aluminium kitchen foil over rough sandpaper, with tacky varnish as an adhesive. After painting I used a little cotton wool for highlights.

[A plan of the Jervis Bay *accompanied E Kilner Berry's article for a waterline model of the ship published in the February 1949 (Vol. 2 No. 14) issue of* Model Ships and Power Boats. *Editor]* ❑

The completed model. Colours are: hull above waterline Aberdeen dark green; yellow funnel; buff masts and derricks.

Photographs by the author.

The Ship Models of the Nurminen Foundation

by Erik Båsk and Alison Moss

In 2007 Conway had the pleasure of working with the John Nurminen Foundation in Helsinki, Finland, on a co-publication, *The History of Seafaring*. The aim of the Foundation is to maintain the cultural heritage and traditions of Finnish seafaring, exploration and cartography. Among their outstanding collections of art, maps and maritime antiques, the Foundation has an impressive collection of ship models on display. A selection of these, ranging from ships of polar expedition to regional types, is described and illustrated in this article for the benefit and interest of *Model Shipwright* readers. For more information, visit the website: www.johnnurminenfoundation.com

Svatoj Pjotr 1733–43

Danish explorer, Vitus Bering's vessels were so-called packets, which were rigged as brigs; that is to say they had two masts equipped with three square sails. The mizzen mast also had a gaff sail and two jibs were attached to the stays of the forebottom. The vessels *Svatoj Pjotr* (*St Peter*) and *Svatoj Pavel* (*St Paul*) were built side by side in Ohotsk on the coast of the Sea of Ohotsk. With the exception of the ships' wooden parts, all the equipment and materi-

The model of *Svatoj Pjotr*.

Adolf Erik Nordenskiöld's *Vega*.

als, from nails to guns (including twenty-eight cannons), were brought through roadless Mother Russia from St Petersburg to Ohotsk. This took several years. The trees necessary for the ships' hulls and rigging were felled in the forests of Kamchatka and were floated across the Sea of Ohotsk to the docks. Bering discovered Alaska in the *Svatoj Pjotr*.

Vega

The Finnish-born explorer, Adolf Erik Nordenskiöld's expedition vessel, the *Vega*, had been built as a whaler in Germany in 1872–3. The *Vega*'s overall length was 43.4 metres, length of the keel 37.6 metres, beam 8.4 metres, depth of the hold 4.6 metres, and cargo-carrying capacity 357 gross register tonnes. The vessel was built of oak, the masts of Oregon pitch pine, and the rigging was supported by steel wire stays. The hull was protected from the ice by a coating made of Greenheart, an Indian hardwood that reached from the level of the chain plates above the waterline to below the waterline about one metre from the keel. To help compensate for the pressure of the ice, the hold was also fitted with iron chests reaching from side to side.

Fram, 1892

In her day *Fram* was the best Polar ship in the world, the only vessel designed to be surrounded by the ice and move with its flow. The Arctic explorer, Fridtjof Nansen, and legendary naval architect and boat builder, Colin Archer, together with another polar explorer and scientist, Otto Sverdrup, followed guidelines based on the experience of native peoples in the ship's design.

Fram's strength was startling: the three-layered side planking was 32.5cm thick on the waterline but taking into consideration the insula-

Model of a flute.

tion between the layers, the sides were between 70cm and 80cm thick.

Fram's main measurements were: overall length 39 metres, waterline length 34.5 metres, length of keel 31 metres, beam at the waterline 10.4 metres, maximum beam 11 metres, average depth 5.25 metres, draught 3.75 metres (with a displacement of 530 tonnes), draught 4.75 metres (with a displacement of 800 tonnes), weight 420 tonnes, maximum cargo 380 tonnes, net register tonnage 402, sail area 600 square metres and 220-horsepower steam engine.

The flute

The common trading vessel type of its time was the seventeenth-century flute. The flute combines a number

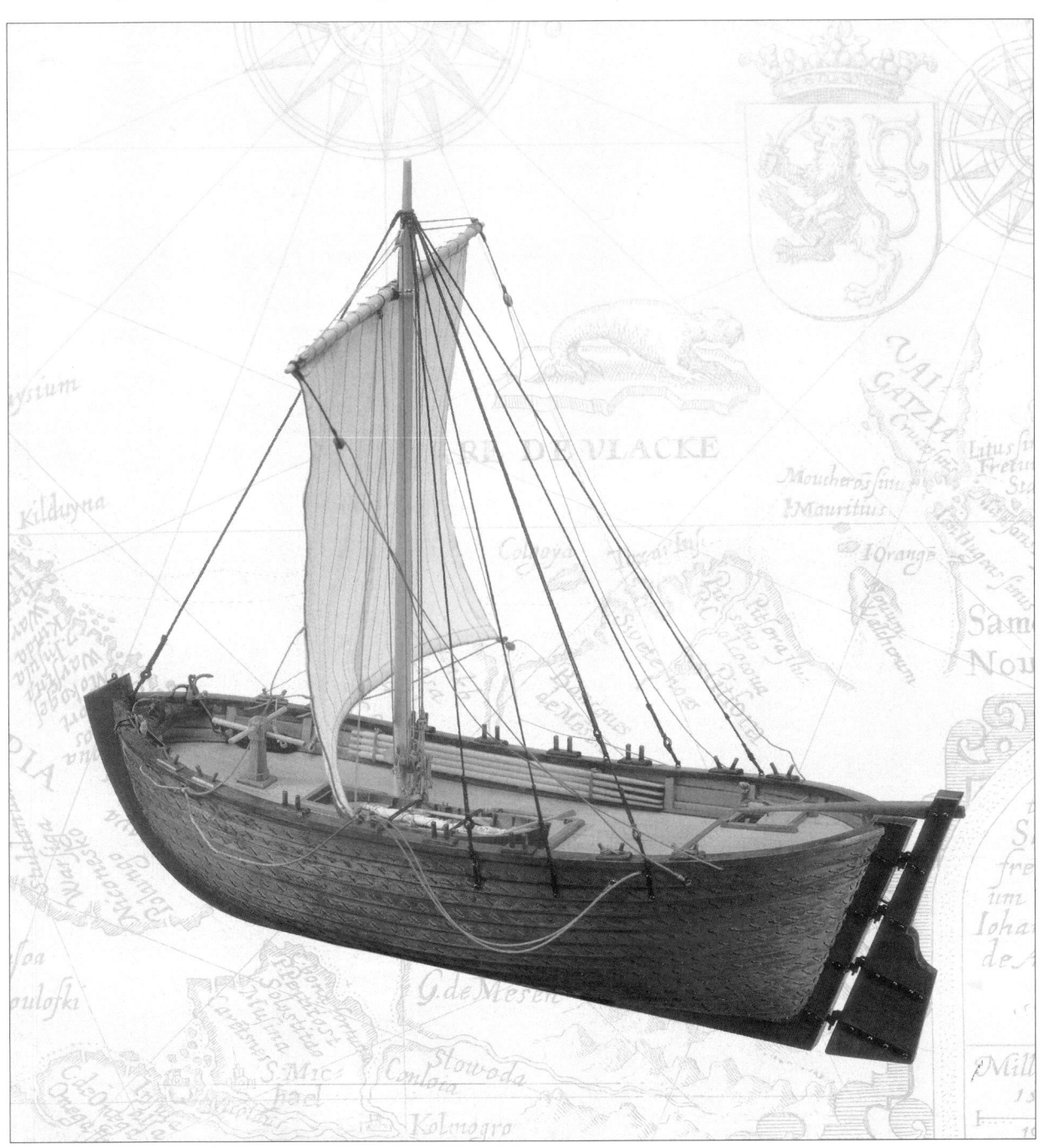

Model of a kotch.

Model of SS *Inkeri Nurminen*. Another rarity at the foundation is a fully restored captain's saloon of SS *Inkeri Nurminen*, built in Hartlepool in 1882. This is on display at the John Nurminen headquarters in Huolintatalo, Helsinki. You can see a picture of this saloon on their website. *Inkeri Nurminen* was completed in 1892 by Furness, Withy & Co. (Lim.), West Hartlepool as *Marie* for Alfred Burdick & John Cook, London.

of advantages: it was cheap to build, easy to sail, its taxable value was low and its deadweight capacity was high. Typical of the flute was its pear-shaped form, wide hold and narrow deck. The flute's popularity was also based on its adaptability; different flute types were developed for transporting different products. Adapted for whaling, the flute had a reinforced bow, strengthened masts and davits along the afterdeck from which the whaling boats were hung on the tackle.

Gjøa

Gjøa was a so-called ordinary yacht, which shipbuilders in the nineteenth century designed to withstand the powerful winds of the North Atlantic coastline. Gjøa was built in Rosendal, west Norway in 1872. The Norwegian, Roald

Amundsen, had become convinced that the most convenient vessel for the Northwest Passage would be a small, light, smooth-sailing ship, with a shallow draught. Gjøa was 23 metres long, 6.6 metres wide, had a draught of 2.5 metres and a net register tonnage of 47. The ship was rigged as a yacht with a gaffsail and topsail and three jibs. In addition, the mast carried a square sail. Amundsen had a combustion engine installed, the first in the history of polar vessels.

HMS *Hecla*, 1815

Many ships used on Arctic expeditions were originally designed for other purposes. Before a voyage, they would be adapted to meet the new demands. In the 1820s William Parry made four voyages in search of the Northwest Passage, all of them

in bomb ketches. HMS *Hecla*, which took part in all four voyages, was the flagship on three occasions. She was about 40 metres long and 10 metres in the beam. The 375-ton *Hecla* was launched at North Barton. She originally had three masts and square rigging. On her fourth voyage, the *Hecla* achieved a new latitude record of the times: 82° 45' North.

The kotch

The kotch was developed as early as the eleventh century on the White Sea coast. In addition to the double layer of planking, particular to the kotch was its half-oval hull. Due to this hull shape, the kotch would 'plop' upwards when squeezed by the ice and thus escape damage.

The kotch had a single sail, probably a square sail. In north-east Siberia, where this vessel was devel-

Another view of the model of SS *Inkeri Nurminen*.   ***Photographs courtesy of the John Nurminen Foundation.***

oped the furthest, a 20-metre long, 6.5-metre wide kotch would have had a single mast and a sail area of some 100 square metres. The maximum speed a kotch is known to have reached is 6.5 knots for five hours.

The lotjas

Lotjas were originally used only on rivers and lakes in Russia, but since the twelfth century, they were also used at sea. For a long time, they were clinker built, but since the turn of the sixteenth century, they started to use the flat seam, especially at the stern. At the same time, they were fitted with three single-pole masts, each with one square sail.

Lotjas were built along the White Sea coastline up until the 1860s. The largest seagoing Lotja was 25–26 metres long, 8 metres wide and had a draught of 2.5 metres and cargo-carrying capacity of 200 tons. ❑

THE HISTORY OF SEAFARING

by Donald Johnson and Juha Nurminen

ISBN 9781844860401
Hardback, 344 pages, 345 x 255mm, £40 illustrated in full colour

• The ultimate single-volume history of seaborne exploration
• 35 feature boxes on ship development and instruments
• Over 250 illustrations, many of which are published for the first time.

Two Cargo Liners

City of Bombay and Clan Shaw

by Robert Wilson

These two cargo liners show the changing style of ships over a period of thirteen years. The first of these two vessels, the *City of Bombay*, was a pre-war design, completed by Barclay, Curle, Glasgow, in 1937 for Ellerman Lines. She was designed for the UK–India route. She was powered by steam turbines driving a single screw. The four furnaces could be fired either by oil or by coal, and the changeover system was quick and uncomplicated. With a gross tonnage of 7,140, the ship had a length of 455ft bp, a breath of 59ft and a

depth of 39ft. She had an enormous crew of about 150 men. The ship had a very short life, being torpedoed and sunk on 13 December 1942 by *U159*. There were 130 survivors, but unfortunately, twenty men out of her total complement were lost.

A general arrangement plan of the *City of Bombay* is to be found on pages 662/663 of the November 1937 issue of *Shipbuilding & Shipping Record*.

I decided on a scale of 1in = 32ft (1:384). In order to obtain a copy of the plan at this scale size I scanned it

into the computer and printed several copies of it at 156.3 per cent enlargement. Several copies were required because I like to use pieces of the plans as templates for the various components of the model.

I used a piece of obeche for the hull. The shape of the hull in those old pre-war ships was usually quite uncomplicated, and the basic shape could be carved quite quickly. In this case the work was facilitated by omitting the poop, bridge and forecastle, which would be added later.

The hull profile is marked on the side of the block, and should be cut first, followed by the outline of the deck. If the process is reversed, the outline of the profile will be lost, and it is difficult to re-mark it on the shaped side of the block. The remainder of the construction followed principles already described in previous articles. However, I am continually changing and improving my methods of construction and materials used.

In recent years, I have found that I have developed allergies to contact adhesive. If I get it on the backs of my fingers where the skin is softer, I develop itchy red weals if I do not remove it within half an hour or so. These can take two or three days to disperse. I have no idea whether this is because of changes in adhesive's formula, or my advancing years. I am finding, too, that I am now adversely affected by the fumes given off by these adhesives. Consequently I have been paying more attention to adhesives that do not affect me. I find that the 'white' wood glue, widely available under a variety of brand names, is harmless to me. Of low odour, it is easily washed off, being water-soluble. It also forms a powerful bond between two wood surfaces.

When bonding plasticard to wood, I have found a non-toxic contact adhesive that works very well. Similar adhesives are no doubt available in other countries.

With the *City of Bombay* model, I decided to cut out all the decks, deckhouses and funnel at the same time. Then I made the seven hatches and placed them all loosely together. This gave me an early indication of how the model would look. One of the photographs shows how I have used spare plan copies to make templates for all the upperworks as well as the main hull.

I had decided on a fairly rough sea setting for this model, so the next task was to make the display case and then cut the inner base to fit. The inner base was then edged with bevelled mahogany and a snugly fitting

wooden tray for the sea assembled. The rough model was placed in the tray, supported at the required angle with six pieces of wood cut to give the hull the required angle of roll and pitch. The hull was held firmly in the tray by two long screws driven up into it from underneath. The Plasticine sea was then fitted and shaped.

More complete details of the base, sea tray, and forming and painting of the sea have already been described by my wife on page 40 of *MS137*. The photographs of page 42 of that issue show the completed sea for the *City of Bombay*.

During the construction of the hull, display case, base and sea, I often break off to work on some of the finer details such as the cargo winches. These were all turned from brass rod and I find that, provided I

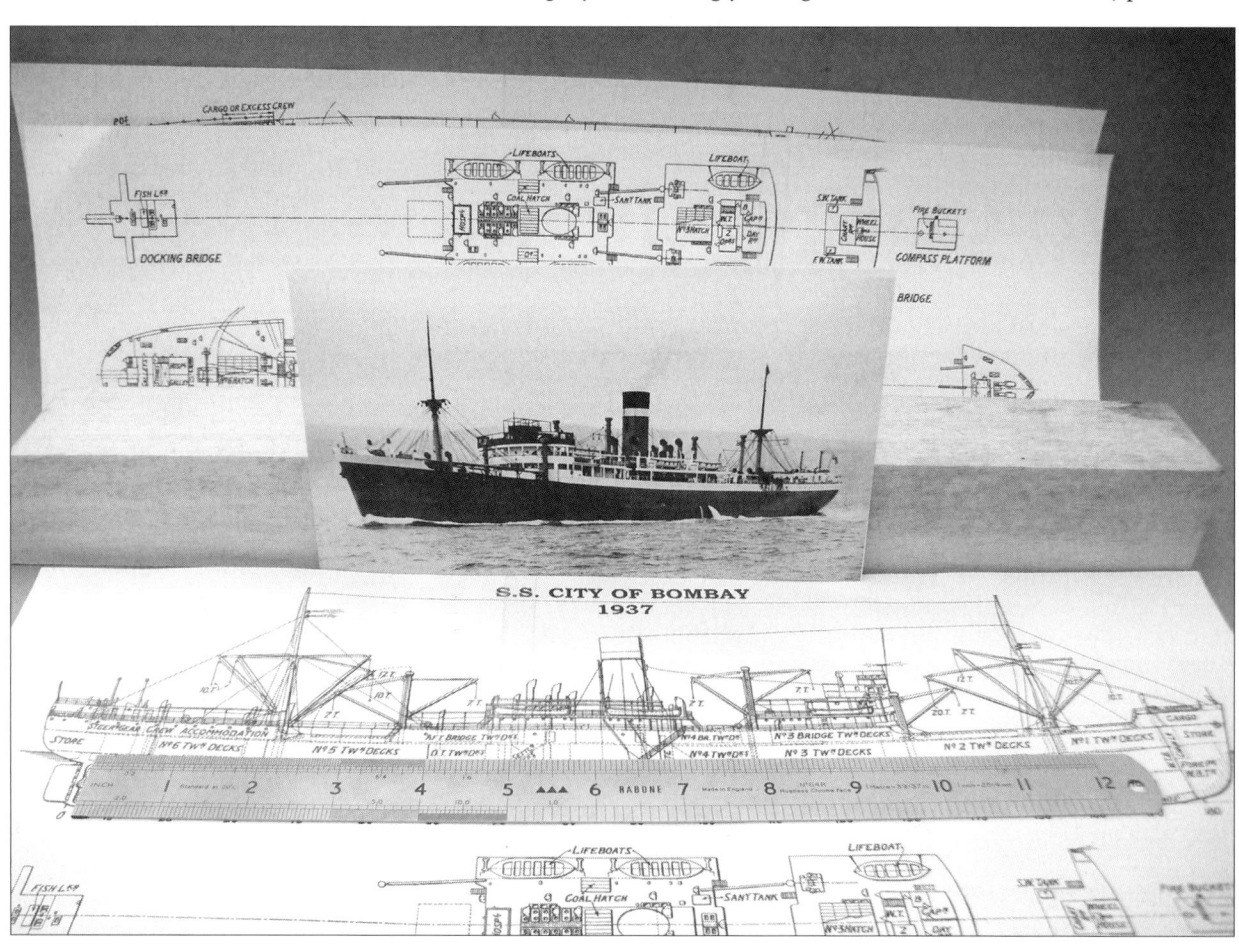

City of Bombay. **Photograph shows plan enlarged to 1:384 scale, and wood selected for hull.**

City of Bombay. **All the main components of the model placed loosely in position.**

am in the right mood, it does not take long to turn all the individual components, which are then assembled on small square pieces of brass shim and finally spray-painted the required colour.

After adding the three raised islands, i.e. the aforementioned poop, bridge amidships and forecastle, the hull was carved to shape.

After being sanded smooth, it was 'plated with strips of paper masking tape. The bare steel decks were painted red oxide; I used a spray can obtained from an automobile shop. It was, of course, necessary to mask off the areas of wooden planking on top of the midship and poop decks while this was done. The hull was then painted using Chromacolour

craft paints. These are water-based, and dry very quickly to a matt finish.

Once this stage has been reached, the model was really taking shape and usually fires up my enthusiasm.

The brass funnel was prepared for painting, after a small plate with a hole drilled in it was soldered across the inside of the bottom to take the small fixing screw.

City of Bombay. **The rough hull with the base ready for the sea.**

City of Bombay. **The sea ready for painting, and the cargo winches under construction.**

The funnel colour was buff with a black top above a white band. The line of the top and bottom edges of the white band were lightly scored into the brass using a small pipe-cutter. The whole of the funnel was then sprayed with white matt primer (automobile supplies). When it was dry, the top two sections were carefully masked off with paper masking tape and the lower part painted buff with aerosol gloss. Finally, the black top section was hand-painted using enamel paint. The score line in the funnel helped greatly with this.

The bridge, wheelhouse and bridge wing cabs were varnished wood. Somehow I have always found it difficult to get this woodwork to look right on miniature models. When browsing around a model shop, I found sheets of white plasticard, faintly scored with lines on one surface. I made up the woodwork from thin strips cut from this sheet, with the lines running vertically. The various pieces were joined using liquid plastic weld. This is specially made for this purpose. I

then carefully sprayed it with gloss maple automobile paint whilst holding it in a pair of surgical clamp forceps. Once dry, I had to touch up the part where the forceps had held it. To do this, I sprayed a small quantity of the paint on to a tin lid and applied it quickly with a fine brush.

None of the deck details were particularly complicated. The lifeboats were vacuum formed as described in a previous issue of *Model Shipwright*. The masts and ventilators were made from brass rod and tube.

For a long time, because I have been experiencing some problems, very similar to those described above, with the particular contact adhesive I use when making and fitting wire rigging, I have been seeking a suitable non-toxic substitute. Eventually I tried a rapid epoxy resin that I had used previously only for display cases and woodwork. By mixing just small quantities at a time, I found that it would remain workable for about ten minutes.

Also, being a thick paste, it would hold rigging in position whilst drying. It does have a slight odour, but nothing like that from contact adhesives. I found, too, that because of its generally unpleasant sticky feeling, should any get on my fingers this was immediately apparent, and being water-based, could be washed off at once.

Usually I complete the display case long before the model is finished. This breaks up the work and makes a pleasant interlude. The method of building cases was described in *MS135*. In that article I mentioned that I veneered the 18mm base quadrant moulding with steamed beech veneer. A number of people have asked me how I do this. The method is quite simple. Timber merchants usually stock moulding with a quarter-circle inner curve. I cut two lengths of this curve and glued them on to a long strip of fairly thick wood to form a half circle with a 18mm radius. In the illustration, the central vertical join is not visible in the photograph, but

City of Bombay. **The model begins to take shape.**

the seam along the bottom of the curve shows how the two lengths are mounted opposite each other to form the convex curve.

Steamed beech, incidentally, is the name of the veneer; I do not steam it. All that needs to be done to make the veneer fit in the jig is to wet it under the tap and wipe off the surplus water. It immediately takes on a slight curve and can be pressed into the jig without any danger of cracking. I then coat the veneer with white wood glue. As this may be thinned with water anyway, it does not matter that the veneer is still damp. In addition, I coat the curved surface of the quadrant with white glue and then clamp it into the jig using a number of clamps, applying quite a considerable pressure on the clamps to ensure that the quadrant is touch-ing the veneer all the way along its length. After about 20 minutes, I remove the clamps. It is usually nec-essary to prize the veneered quadrant carefully out of the jig using a screw-driver inserted beneath one of the ends. Because of the pressure exerted by the clamps, it seems that a small amount of glue usually seeps through the veneer and begins to form a bond with the curved surface of the jig. It is

City of Bombay. **The wooden bridge, chartroom and cabins in position.**

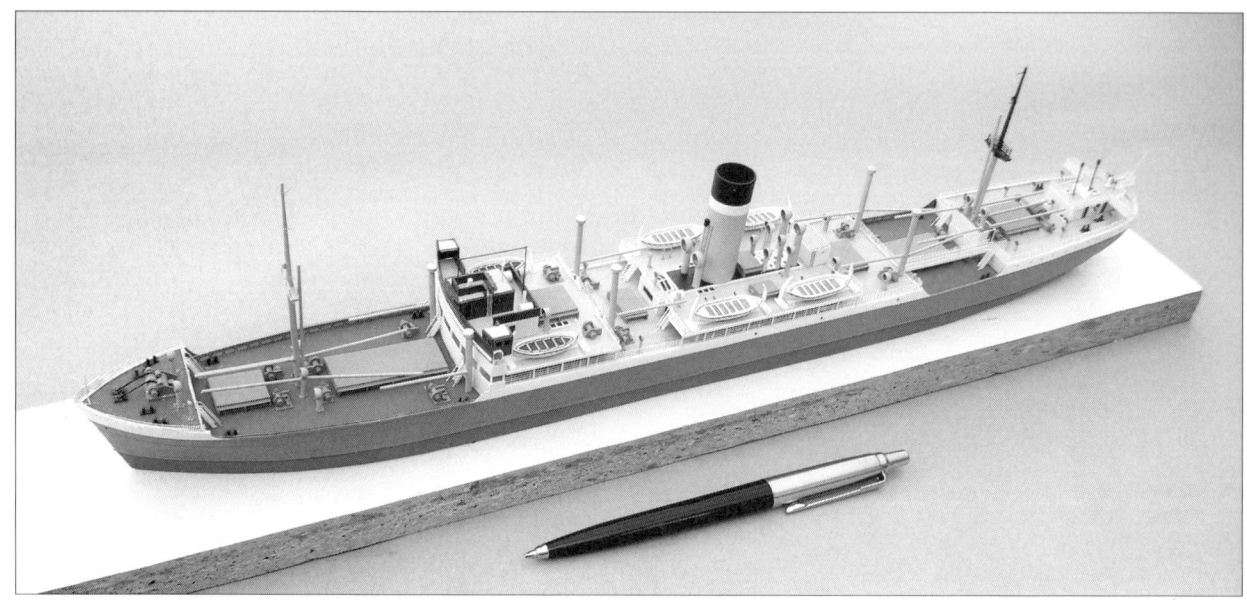

City of Bombay. The completed hull awaiting rigging.

therefore necessary to prize the quadrant free before it becomes too firmly fixed. Once removed, I let it dry properly before trimming off the excess veneer from side and ends.

Because of the early preparation of the display case, base and sea, I was able to fit the model into the sea when the rigging had been completed. In the photograph of the finished model without the display case, it will be seen that I laced a piece of veneered quadrant along the front of the model to hide the rough front side of the base.

City of Bombay. Discarded tin lids make useful disposable palettes.

City of Bombay. The curved wood
sections facing each other.

The sea base is glued on to a sheet
of thick card that has been covered
with green felt. I drill three holes in
each of the long sides. When the display case is fitted over the model, it
rests on the shelf formed by the felt-
covered card. To secure the model in
the case, I drive six woodscrews up
through the fixing holes. As long as
the model is firmly fixed in its sea and
the sea base is firmly glued to the
green felt-covered base, it is quite
safe to turn it upside down to do this.
All the screws are countersunk and
are covered by square patches of self-
adhesive green felt.

Clan Shaw

The second model is the cargo liner
Clan Shaw, built in 1950, thirteen
years after the *City of Bombay*.

The *Clan Shaw* was the first of
four sister-ships, and was designed

City of Bombay. Damp veneer pressed into the curve.

for the same service as the *City of Bombay,* trading mainly between the UK and India. The other three were *Clan Sinclair, Clan Sutherland* and *Clan Stewart.* She was a general cargo liner of 8,700 gross tons, built for Cayzer, Irvine Ltd (Clan Line) by the Greenock Dockyard Company. She had a length of 512.6ft overall, 488.75ft bp, a beam of 66.5ft and a depth of 28ft. Accommodation was fitted for twelve passengers.

In 1960, the *Clan Shaw* was transferred to the newly formed Springbok Line and renamed *Steenbok.* A year later, she was transferred to Safmarine and re-named *South African Seafarer.* Shortly afterwards, the name was shortened to *S.A. Seafarer,* a retrograde step in my view. In 1966, the *S.A. Seafarer* went ashore near the Green Point Lighthouse, Cape Town, when manoeuvring in bad weather. It was not long before she began to break up. Several days later, I arrived in Cape Town aboard the Union-Castle flagship RMS *Windsor Castle.* A number of us went along to Green Point where we became witness to the sad end of the *S.A Seafarer* ex *South African Seafarer,* ex *Clan Shaw.* Broken into three pieces by that time, she was relentlessly being pounded to pieces.

Clan Line vessels were generally of clean, attractive lines and their good looks were improved by the contrasting colour scheme. This was: red oxide below water, pink along the waterline with black topsides beneath a white band extending the full length of the hull.

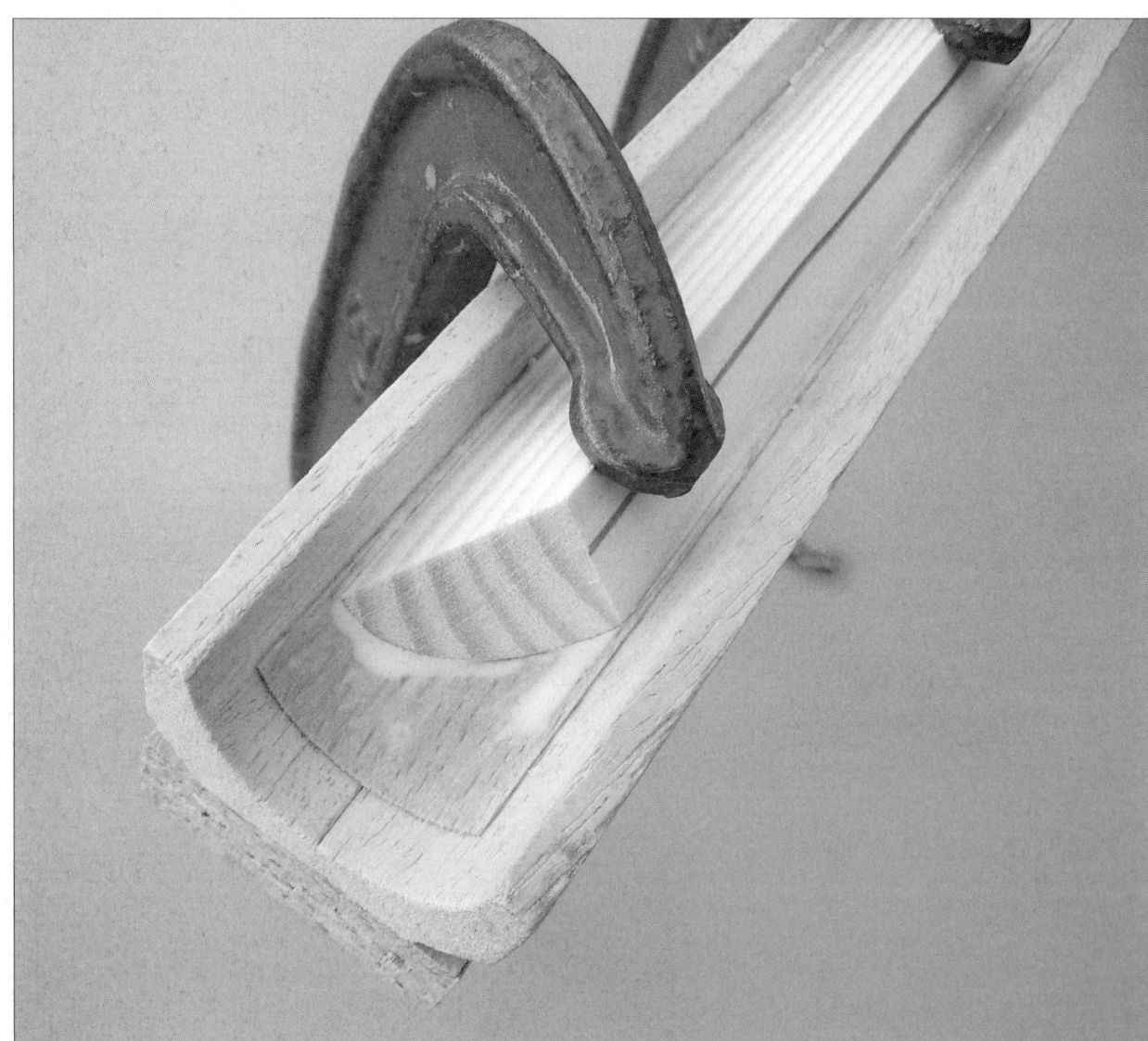

City of Bombay. **The 18mm quadrant clamped in the jig.**

1937 CITY OF BOMBAY 1942
Ellerman Lines Ltd
Great Britain

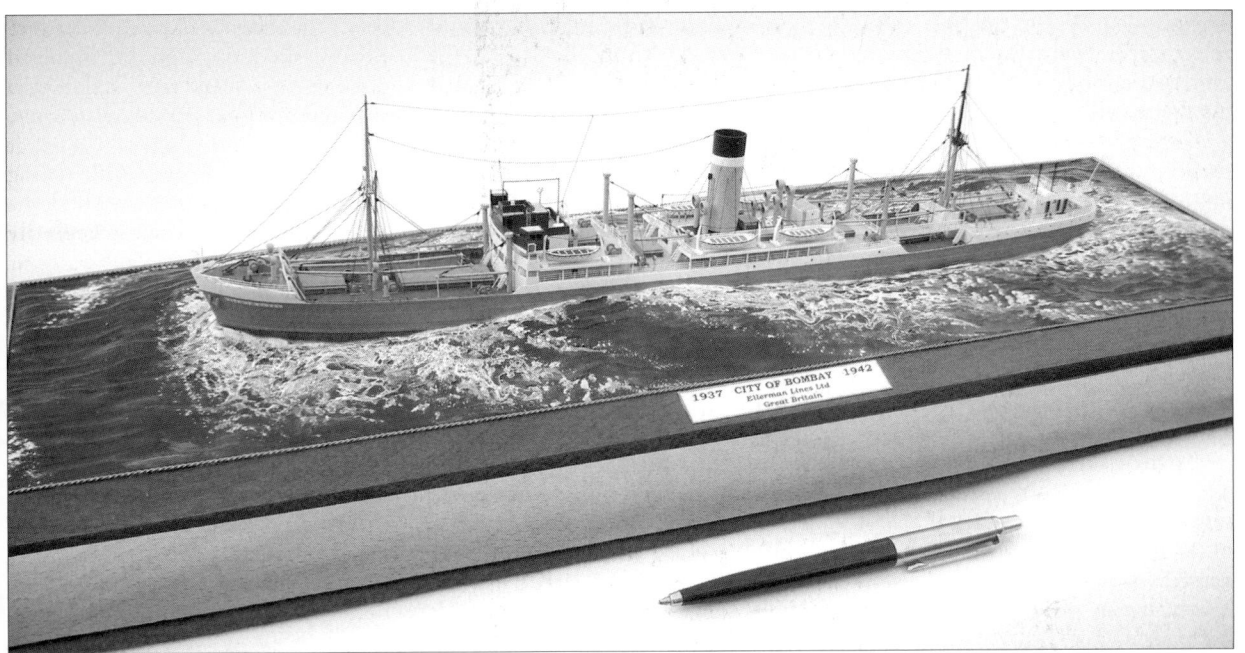

City of Bombay. The completed model fitted into the sea.

The model

A general arrangement plan of the *Clan Shaw* was published in the January 1950 issue of *The Shipping World*. In order to adjust the size to 1in = 32ft (1:384), I scanned it into the computer and printed it at 161 per cent.

I decided to make this model with a full hull. The work difference between a waterline model and a full hull is about the same as far as time

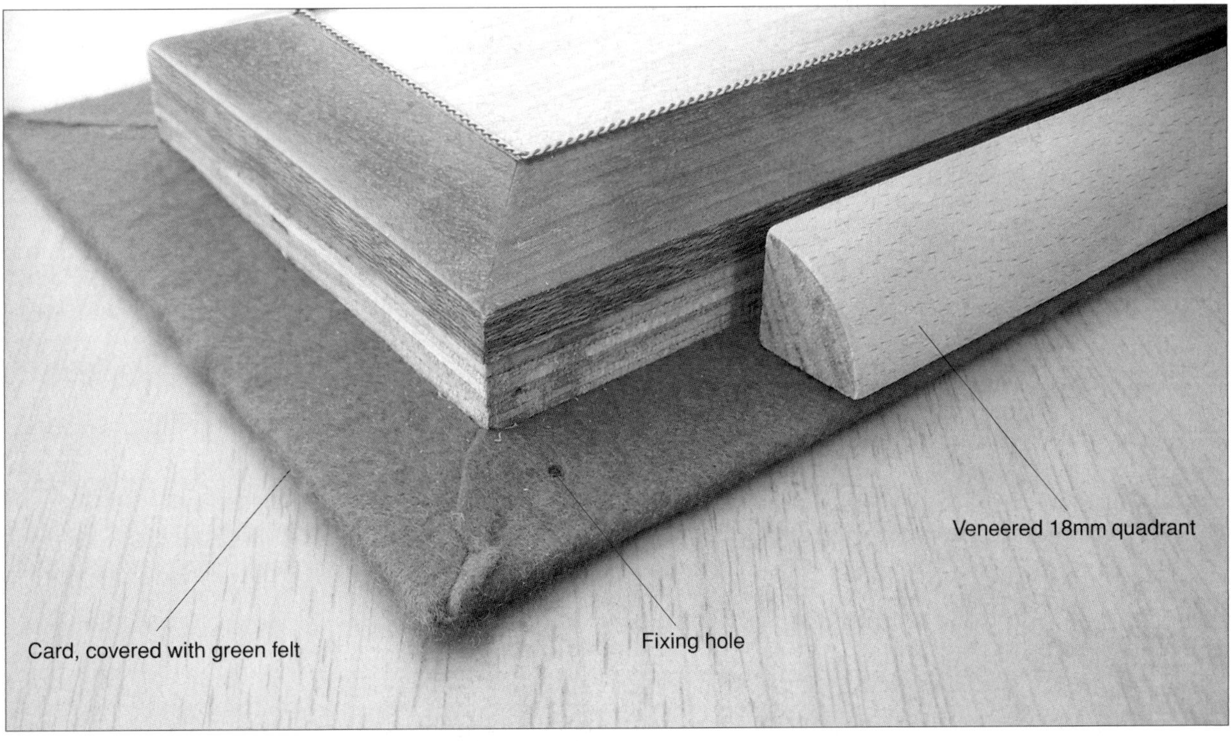
Veneered 18mm quadrant
Card, covered with green felt
Fixing hole

City of Bombay. Showing how the display case is fixed to the base.

is concerned. With a full hull no sea is required, being replaced by the underwater body of the hull including the propeller and rudder.

General construction of the model followed my usual practices, but as it is a full-hull one, some notes on work on the underwater part of the hull may be of interest.

I rarely find a lines plans accompanying the general arrangement drawings published in the technical journals. So in most cases, I carve the hulls by eye. By cutting stem and stern inserts from thin brass sheet and gluing them into slots at each end of the hull, I am assured of getting the correct profile. Hull shapes of the type of ship I build are all very similar. To put it very simply, below the waterline they are pointed at both ends. The bow insert is very easy as it is just a simple shape cut out and glued in position in a slot cut in the bow. The stern insert is a bit

more complicated. I make a copy of the stern profile from the plan, to the same scale as the model, and paste it on a thin sheet of brass. I cut round it including the rudder. The propeller aperture is also cut out and a narrow slot cut forward of this to take the stern tube (and to allow entry and exit of a jeweller's saw blade). The stern tube is made from a piece of small diameter brass tube, which is soldered into this slot. I complete most of the hull shaping before fitting the stern insert as its absence makes this a little easier. It is when the hull is almost the required shape that I fit the stern insert, and fair in any gaps with plastic metal.

The method of making the propeller is as follows. I start by drawing the shape of the propeller, in this case a four-bladed one, on a large sheet of paper, scan it into the computer, and reduce it to the size required. This is then stuck on to a

very thin sheet of brass and cut out. Because the brass is so thin it can be done using a small pair of nail scissors, with a final trimming up done with a small cutting wheel in a hand-held miniature electric drill. (Note: use protective goggles when doing this as the small cutting wheels are liable to shatter from time to time. Although they do not disintegrate with any great force, it is better to be safe than sorry.) After the blades have been cut out, I solder them to a short length of brass rod, which will fit into the stern tube. A conical boss is then either glued or soldered centrally on the after end of the mounted propeller blades. They may then be twisted to the required angle. I do not glue a propeller into position until the model is otherwise complete. It is very delicate and easily damaged if fitted too early.

On the upper deck short lengths of steel bulwarks were fitted on each

The S.A. *Seafarer* some weeks after she was wrecked at Cape Town in 1966.

Figure 1. Stern of the *Clan Shaw* as shown on the profile.

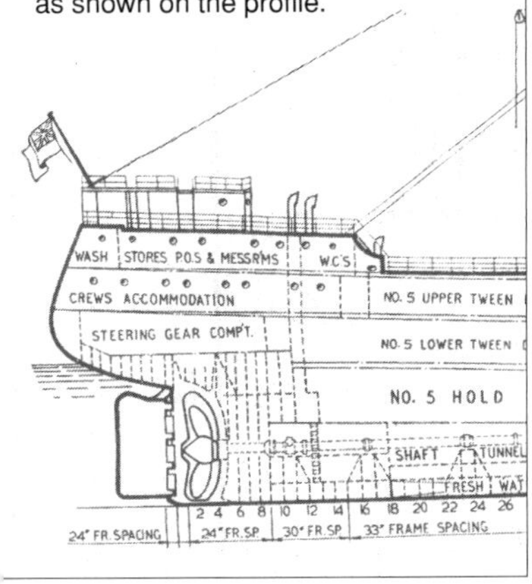

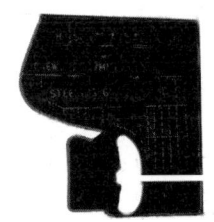

WASH
STORES P.O.S & MESSRMS
W.C'S
CREWS ACCOMMODATION
NO. 5 UPPER TWEEN
STEERING GEAR COMPT.
NO. 5 LOWER TWEEN
NO. 5 HOLD
SHAFT
TUNNEL
FRESH
WAT
2 4 6 8 10 12 14 16 18 20 22 24 26
24" FR. SPACING
24" FR. SP.
30" FR. SP.
33" FRAME SPACING

Figure 2. Stern brass insert ready to have stern tube fitted.

Figure 3. The propeller.

POOP DECK
DOCKING BRIDGE
WHEELHOUSE TOP
NAV. BRIDGE
BOAT DECK
BRIDGE DECK
FORECASTLE DECK
BOAT DECK
FUNNEL
ENGINE ROOM
BOILER ROOM
NO. 3 HOLD
WHEEL HOUSE

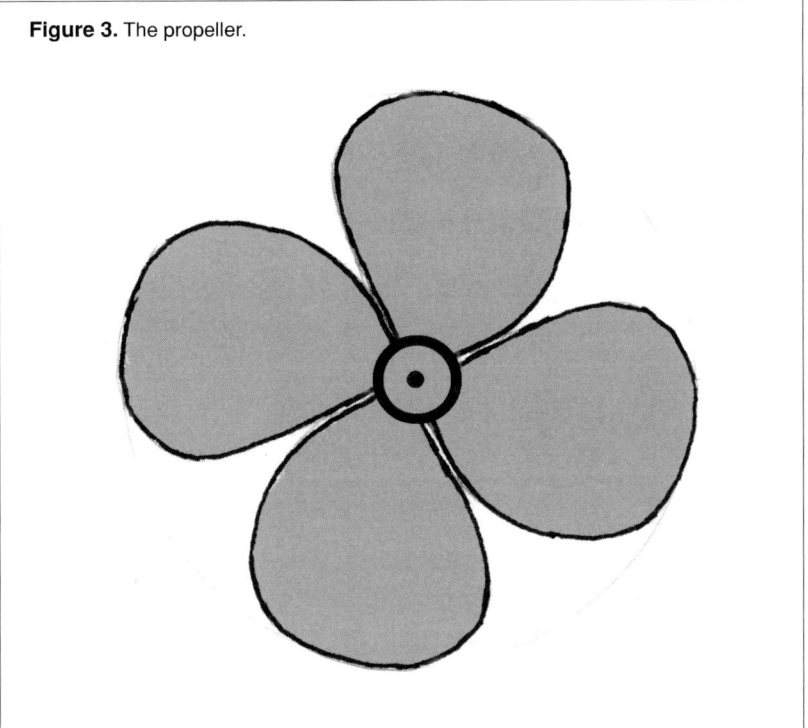

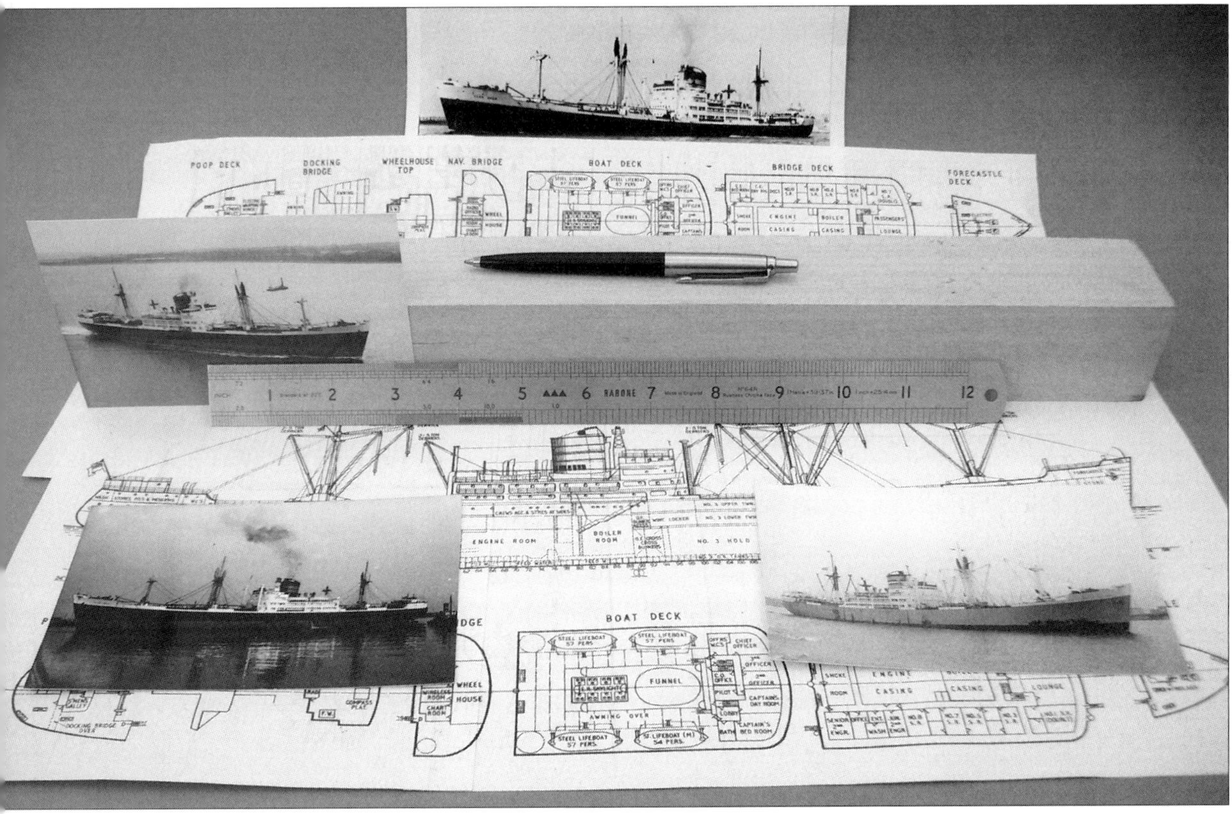

Clan Shaw. The enlarged G A plan, together with the wood blocks all ready for building to start.

Clan Shaw. Basic superstructure ready to have the finer details fitted.

side abreast the masts, which simplified fitting the guardrails as no long lengths were required.

The accommodation structure was rather more complicated than that of the *City of Bombay*. It was built up in the same way, with white plasticard facing on the individual blocks. The portholes were done with a small drill bit. The windows were done on the computer and printed on shiny, self-adhesive film and fixed in position. This is very effective as the windows have a shine to them.

The funnel of the *Clan Shaw* and her sister-ships was fitted with an open cowl for the purpose of smoke

deflection. Making this on a small scale initially needed a great deal of experimentation. The eventual solution was simple in the extreme. I began with a normal flat-topped shape. The basic funnel was made from brass tubing of a diameter that, when squeezed, would provide a workpiece having the correct cross-sectional length and breadth of the funnel. The first task was to score a ring round it at the level of the top red band, and again at the bottom of the lower red ring. This was done by using a small pipe cutter. This is a great aid to the painting. I then squeezed the tube into the correct oval shape in a vice. This operation

made the sides slightly concave, but the distortion was so slight that I was able to correct it with a smooth file.

A thin strip of brass with a hole in the centre was soldered across the inside of the bottom of the funnel to allow it to be screwed on the model at a later stage.

A thin oval wire ring was made to the exact shape of the funnel top. The after part of the wire oval was spot soldered to the back of the

Figure 4. *Clan Shaw's* funnel as shown on the plan.

Figure 5. Start with a flat plain top to the funnel.

Figure 6. An oval-shaped wire ring is added to the funnel top, the raised fore end supported by a small piece of thin plasticard.

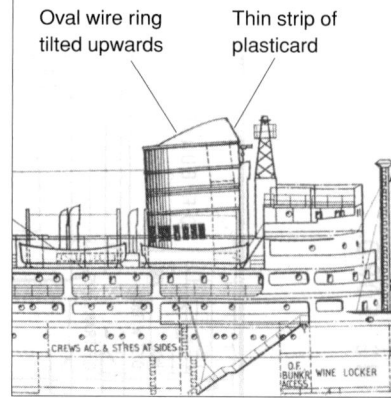

Oval wire ring tilted upwards

Thin strip of plasticard

Clan Shaw. Rigging completed, and model ready to be put into the display case.

funnel top, whilst the forward part of it was raised to the required angle, held with a thin strip of plasticard glued in position.

I wrapped a thin piece of copper wire round a drill shank and cut off a circle of wire which I then cut in half. These halves were glued beneath the raised wire funnel ring in the required position. The gap behind the half-rings was filled in with a clear membrane. The material I used for this is called *Micro Kristal Klear*, obtained in a small bottle from a local model shop. It looks

like white wood glue. If it is applied to one end of a small open area it can be drawn across to form a thin membrane that dries clear. Its real use is to form small, clear windows. When it had dried, I painted it black; the sequence is shown in Figures 4–9. The funnel colours for *Clan Line* vessels are quite simple: black funnel with two red bands; the area between upper and lower bands is black. First of all, I painted the top and bottom of the funnel black, using the scored marks as a painting guide. When dry I painted the inbe-

tween area red. I then cut a thin strip of black-painted film and glued it round the middle of this section to form two separate red bands of equal width.

Located just forward of the funnel was a radar scanner set on the top of a short four-sided lattice-work structure. The scanner itself was enclosed in a circular acrylic dome. I could not see any way of making a latticework structure at this scale, so I just included the four side supports and left the lattice-work to the imagination.

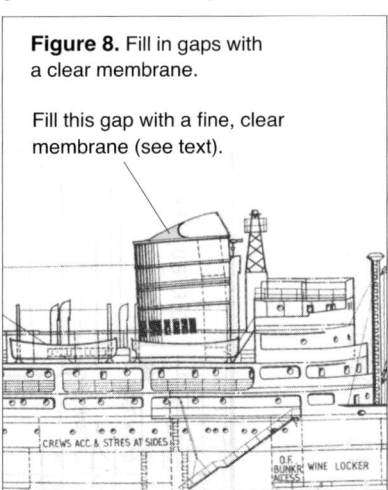

Figure 7. Supporting rings glued in place.

Half of a thin copper wire ring glued in on either side of funnel

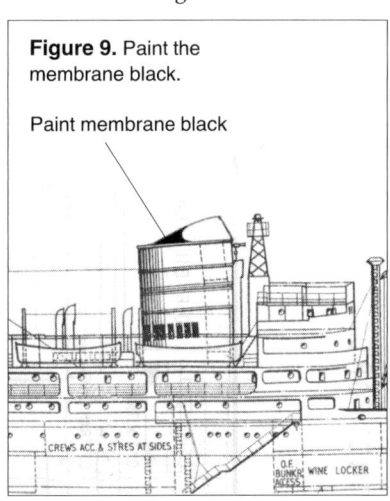

Figure 8. Fill in gaps with a clear membrane.

Fill this gap with a fine, clear membrane (see text).

Figure 9. Paint the membrane black.

Paint membrane black

Clan Shaw. **The completed model.**

Photographs by the autho

When I build a full-hull model of a steam or motor ship, I usually have the derricks raised and rigged as this gives a more interesting overall picture. Also, I feel justified in leaving off the radio aerials. If these are rigged between the mastheads, they can be quite difficult to fit in larger models, and be vulnerable to damage.

In full-hull models, the veneer that I place beneath the hull is steamed beech. This provides a goo contrast with the bevelle mahogany edging and the steame beech woodwork of the display case The nameplate was produced on th computer.

USS *Olympia*

by W G Ballenger

Not so long ago Bluejacket Shipcrafters of Seaport, Maine, produced a very high-quality, limited edition (200 only) kit of the famous American warship USS *Olympia,* the navy's oldest steel ship still afloat. I was then asked by a friend to build him one of these kits.

To develop the plans and components for the kit model of *Olympia,* Bluejacket had access to contemporary Bureau of Construction and Repair drawings, ordnance manuals, and photographs. The scale of the model is ³⁄₃₂in = 1ft (1:128), and it shows the ship as she was in 1895.

Olympia was built by the Union Iron Works, Seattle, California, being launched in 1892, and commissioned early in 1895. She had a long and varied career, taking part in operations all over the world. She is now preserved, and berthed in Philadelphia. The main details, as built, are:

Length: 344ft 1in.
Breadth: 53ft 0in.

Draft: 21ft 6in.
Speed: 20 knots.
Displacement: 5596 tons.
Armament: 4 8in/30; 10 5in/40
  4 6pdr; 6 1pdr; 5 18in torped
  tubes.

The model

The solid wood hull came partly fin ished, and this was completed to th final shape, using the templates sup plied to ensure accuracy. Th instruction book was satisfactory and well illustrated. The quality o the fittings and etched items wa excellent. It took me some 240 hour to build the model.

(Note: a detailed account of th ship's activities and varied career ca be found in the *Dictionary of Ameri can Naval Fighting Ships,* 1970, Vol 5, pp. 152-153).

Fore deck detai

Broadside view of completed model.

Midships, showing boat stowage. The funnels were yellow-buff with black top.

After deck detail.

Photographs by the author.

Paddle Tug *Fredrina (c.1900)*

by George Cowie

This was my fourth ship model but the first to be scratch-built. It took some seven years to build. It was done with a little experience, a lot of research, a few hand tools, a vibro-saw, and determination. Then, in year six, I had to take care not to disturb the spider that took up residence.

Fredrina is based on *Model Maker* plans for a 1:32 scale tug *Chieftain*. This iron paddle tug was built in 1899 by J T Eltringham, South Shields, with engine supplied by T Hepple, South Shields. Her dimensions were: length on waterline 108.4ft, breadth moulded 18.8ft, depth 9.9ft. I made a few minor alterations, including a modification to the bow to incorporate a bow rudder, which I felt (hopefully) could improve manoeuvrability, thereby suiting my ideas for making it an effective working model.

Before I started building I purchased almost all of the equipment, which would end up inside the hull. I wanted to make sure it would all go in. Most of the gear is arguably now outdated, more effective and physically smaller items now being readily available.

Like most modelmakers I hoard bits of wood, metal and plastic, of which various bits have been recycled into *Fredrina*.

The model

This was built to a scale of 1:32, and had the following dimensions: length overall, including the 50mm extension to the bow, 1105mm (43.5in), length on waterline including extension 1050mm (41.3in), breadth moulded 176mm (7in), breadth over sponsons 352mm (13.8in), height amidships bottom of keel to deck at side 106mm (4.2in), draught 90mm (3.5in), displacement in full working

The spider that took up residence in year six.

The model is almost completed.

Showing example of riveted plating, and the simulated chequer-plated steps.

order 7.54kg (just under 17lb).

The hull is constructed of 5mm x 2mm obeche planking on ten formers cut from 6mm plywood. With hindsight I wish I had used three more formers. I would have put two amidships in the main hatch area for increased rigidity, and an extra one to strengthen the extension I made to the bow to let me fit a bow rudder. The two extra formers amidships would have strengthened the gunwales, making it safer when lifting the model.

The 50mm extension to the bow, which I considered necessary to facilitate fitting the proposed bow rudder, was done when the basic hull had been completed.

I chose to use relatively thick planks to allow for much sanding down, if needed, to obtain a smooth and shapely hull. The method of bending the planks was as follows: first they were soaked, then run round the heater barrel of a soldering iron while using finger pressure to obtain the desired curvature and twists. It is better to use the 'little and often' technique. Allowing the plank to rest too long on the iron results in scorching, which hardens the wood and makes further bending difficult. When the planking had been completed and well rubbed down to a satisfactory finish, I fitted a bilge keel each side of the hull. These were 36.5cm long, 10mm deep, and made of two thicknesses of 4mm plywood. They were secured to the hull with epoxy glue and from inside the hull with brass screws through three of the formers. It was hoped that these would help to reduce rolling.

I reasoned that it was better to seal the inside of the hull with resin than to apply it to the outside, which would have meant more sanding down. I brush-coated the inside of the hull with glass fibre finishing mat and resin. I could have omitted the glass mat as obeche is so open grained the resin would have penetrated enough to waterproof, seal and strengthen it. I am not in favour of the practice of coating the interior of a hull by pouring in a quantity of resin and sloshing it about. As the resin becomes viscous pockets of air may be trapped in corners; I prefer to brush the resin well into all such places.

After deciding on their size and positions, the main deck access hatches were framed with 6mm square spruce.

To construct the sponsons two 6mm square spruce beams were installed across the hull, extending to the full width of the sponsons. Two 2mm plywood formers, shaped to conform to the inboard sides of the paddle boxes and associated deckhouses were fitted to the inside

Additional shaft bearings.

The seven access hatches have been removed.

surface of the hull. They extend about 12mm down into the hull, and serve to strengthen the hull where the paddle shafts pass through it.

The engine room superstructure, companion ways, etc., fit over the outside of the 10mm high by 1mm thick ply coamings.

Next I cut and fitted a 1mm ply sub-deck in easy-to-cut and handle sections. These were given two coats of varnish on the underside before being fitted in place. The joints were sealed and the deck was sanded down to a smooth camber. I used 2mm ply for the deck margin boards, and 5mm x 2mm obeche for the planking. Dark grey acrylic paint was used to simulate the caulking, rather than black, which looks unnatural. Care must be taken when applying acrylic, for if it gets in the wrong place it is almost impossible

to remove. It is not a good choice; acrylics dry very hard and any lumps must be removed before fitting a plank or it may distort the plank spacing. Two hull compartments were filled with bubble wrap and sealed off, to provide emergency buoyancy.

I did consider making the faces of the paddle boxes removable to facilitate access to the wheels. However, I opted for a more solid job, because I felt that the projection of the boxes made them very vulnerable. The bridge wings are a tight fit on the tops of the paddle boxes, which helps stiffen the whole assembly.

The bulwarks, 20mm high above deck, were made of 1mm plywood, and were screwed to the shadows and epoxy glued to the formers and the sub-deck.

The funnel was made from a redundant bathroom sealant tube,

and the bezels at the top and bottom were originally part of a replaced shower control unit. A smoke generator and its pack of five AA cells are housed in the funnel. An adjacent on/off switch is mounted on the boiler room cover.

So far as deck fittings such as lifeboats, ventilators, bollards, anchors and anchor cable, binnacle, engine room telegraphs, ship's wheel, tow hook, lifebuoys and portholes were concerned, these were purchased, but only after much searching to locate those of the right size and suitability.

The steps on the paddle boxes were formed from 6mm x 6mm obeche cornice moulding carefully chamfered to follow the changing angles of the paddle boxes. These gave an adequate surface area for gluing to the boxes. The treads of all steps were finished off by adding pieces of plastic parcel strapping, which gives a chequered steel plate effect.

Removable companionways, wheelhouse and engine room casing were made from 1mm ply, and then planked with thin mahogany strips. Glazing was thin, clear plastic; one companionway was painted dark blue on the inside. Hinges were of thin brass wire glued in position, and door handles were spherical headed dressmaker pins.

The outside of the hull and appropriate parts of the superstructure were 'steel plated' using self-adhesive plasticised stationery labels. These labels come in a variety of sizes, so it was easy to minimise cutting waste. I examined steel plating on photographs of real ships and read everything I could find in back numbers of *Model Shipwright*. I marked out the run of the strakes of plating on the hull using a soft pencil

and a length of thin plastic strip.

The strakes were fitted on the in-and-out principle. Plates were joggled, and the top, overlap, edge of any plate was marked for riveting. It was essential to cut the under strake of plating correctly, as the overlapping plates, when stuck in place, need to be coaxed with a fingernail to form a realistic joggle.

This was followed by two thin coats of varnish; labels will not stick too well to absorbent surfaces. I made a jig out of thin, stiff card, marking the rivet spacing along two edges at the correct distance in from the edge and pierced a hole at each rivet position. I took a lot of care with this as the rivets need to be uniform to look realistic.

I cut each label (plate) to shape and size, leaving the backing paper in place, and allowing for appropriate riveting overlaps.

I laid it backing side up, on a self-

healing cutting mat then, using the jig and a redundant ballpoint pen, I pressed and rotated the ballpoint at each rivet position hole, thus forming a round pimple on the face side. I did not form rivets where the plate was to be under an adjacent plate. I removed the backing paper and fixed the plate in position on the hull. When the hull and superstructure plating was completed I applied two thin coats of varnish before the final coats of paint. I recommend practising before going on to the real thing. I have tried this technique before and it has proved to be both durable and waterproof.

I should add that a few plates on the superstructure lifted at the edges (due to my carelessness), but as this looked quite realistic, as if the plates were slightly buckled, I left them alone.

The two Como low rpm, high torque motors with adjustable

Bridge and funnel detail.

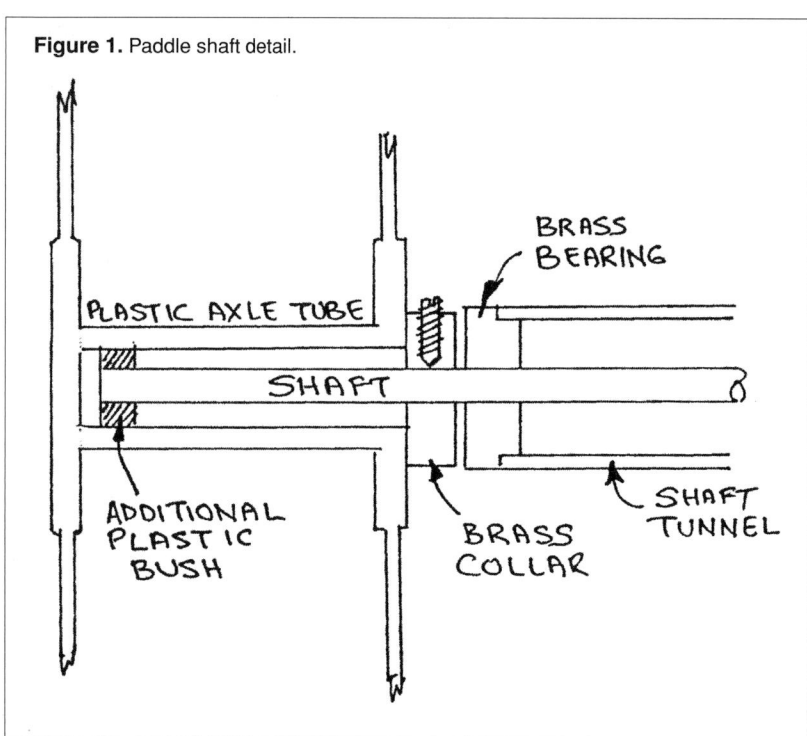

Figure 1. Paddle shaft detail.

PLASTIC AXLE TUBE

BRASS BEARING

SHAFT

ADDITIONAL PLASTIC BUSH

BRASS COLLAR

SHAFT TUNNEL

multi-range epicyclical pile gearboxes allowed experiments on choice of gear ratios during bath trials to determine the maximum paddle speed, under load, which proved to be approximately 72 rpm. It was not possible to calculate the optimum gear ratio due to insufficient data for the on-load motor speed. The final drive is by toothed cog and drive belts. The final ratios were 3:1 on the gearboxes and 40:18 on the toothed drive.

Care must be taken when selecting motors, gearboxes, cog wheels and drive shafts to ensure they all have appropriate, compatible shaft diameters.

Because of the overall length of the motor/gearbox units and the internal width of the hull, the port motor drives the starboard paddle and vice versa.

The paddle wheels are lightweight, plastic, self feathering, made

Stern detail.

by Graupner. They are 140mm diameter by 65mm wide, with eight floats per wheel. I rejected the idea of constructing them of brass, feeling that they would be too heavy. The paddle drive shafts are in brass shaft tunnels, with plain bearings. There is a lubrication hole in each tube, accessed from removable plastic car number plate fixing bolts screwed into the deck.

The shafts run through a brass collar on the inboard side of each paddle wheel and are secured by a grub screw. The width of the wheel can create a lot of strain on a single point fixing. I made the shafts long enough to run through the plastic axle tube and fitted a plastic bush to the end, see Figure 1.

There are seven removable access hatches on deck, all secured in place in appropriate ways. These hatches provide access as follows:

a) fore deck and steering wheel –
bow rudder pulley.
b) forward companion way – bow rudder servo.
c) engine room/bridge structure – drive motors, gearboxes and belt drives.
d) boiler room/funnel – all batteries, R/X, speed controllers, electronics.
e) After companionway, held on with a rubber bungee – switch panel and trimming adjustments on speed controllers.
f) tow rope cradle – stern rudder servo.
g) aft deck – stern rudder pulley.

The equipment is mounted on four separate removable boards. Three boards are fixed to the hull frames and serve to hold the sheet lead ballast in place. The total lead ballast weight is 2.02kg, which is distributed along the hull to minimise pitching.

a) The forward board carries the two
motor/gearbox units mounted on two pieces of heavy gauge aluminium angle. This board is removable through the central hatch after removing the central board and the main battery.

b) The central board carries a 6-volt, 4-ah battery which is recharged on board and a secondary board on which is mounted the electronic control gear. The battery can be removed after removing the central board.

c) The secondary board carries five items of electronic gear and the R/X battery. Each item is clipped into a length of PVC electrical trunking, the sides of which are cut back to give a firm grip to each item. The wiring and servo leads are neatly run in separate lengths of trunking.

d) The aft board can be unscrewed and slid forward after removing the central board. It carries both

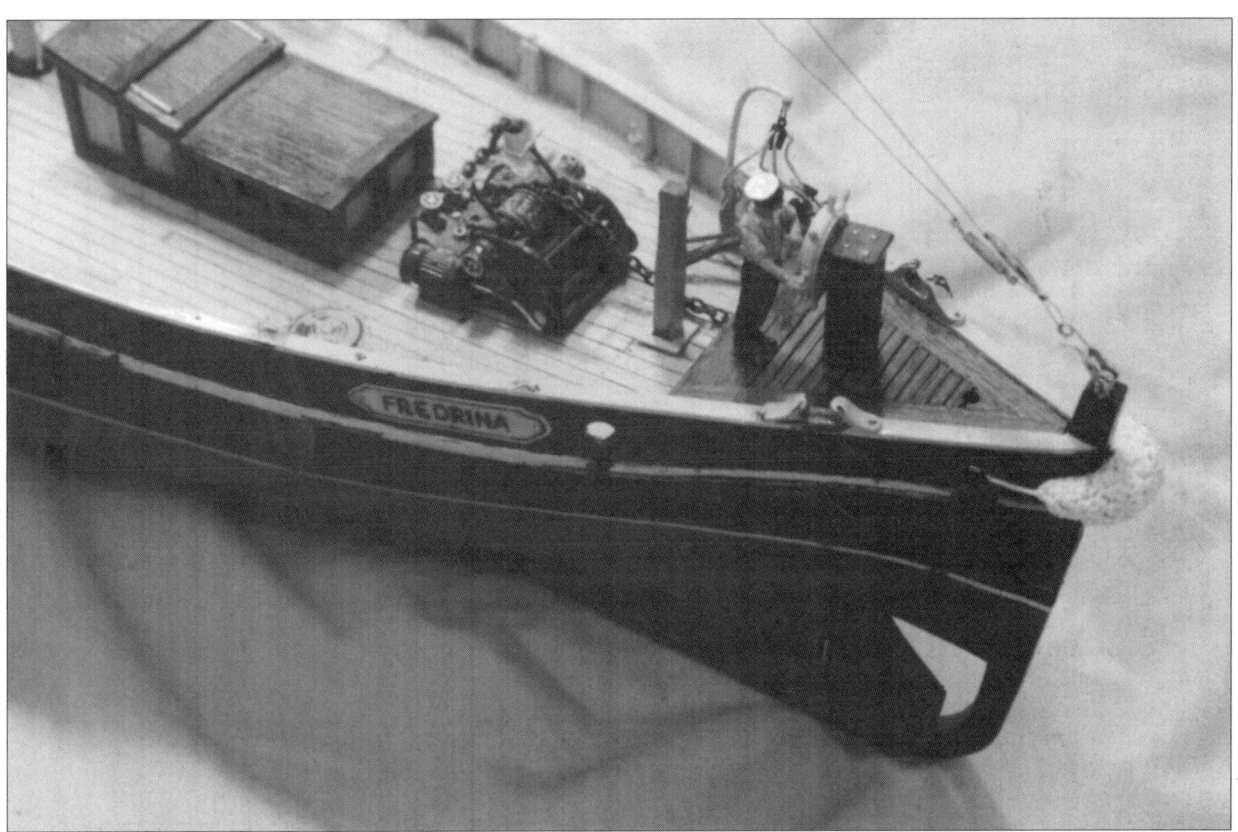

The adder bow rudder, and some fore deck detail.

Bridge detail.

speed controllers underneath the aft deck.

To remove a paddle wheel I have to remove the toothed wheels on the drive shafts, slacken the Allen screws on the paddle wheel collars and remove the feathering crank spigots. I can then slide both shafts to the same side, giving just enough clearance to remove the opposite paddle wheel. I am considering forming two more access hatches by removing some of each paddle box where it is covered by the bridge wings. This would facilitate loosening the locating collar on drive shafts from above, allowing removal of the wheels. At the moment I only have access to the Allen screw from below, a bit of a nightmare.

The crew were made from a 1:35 scale French Foreign Legion plastic kit. The slight difference in scale is hardly seen. Major surgery to some

of the limbs resulted in the desired poses. Cutting down the Legionnaires' caps and adding a cardboard disc produced a realistic sailor's cap. I carved off military items, abraded the surface to get a texture effect and finished off with various colours of acrylic paint. The crew are nailed to the deck through their feet and backed up by epoxy. Where a crewman is holding on to a wheel or a rail, he is 'handcuffed' to it with thin brass wire. It is important to choose crew poses which suggest interaction or movement. The captain's cat just appeared on board one day.

While I admire the care most modelmakers lavish on superb paint finishes, *Fredrina* was always intended to be a working model of a working tug. I ended up by deliberately adding a few dents, scratches and rust patches. The rust patches and streaks were made with cotton wool buds and a sepia-coloured

Brush Pen (I use a Faber Castell, Pitt Artist Pen B, which is virtually permanent). I touch the brush on to the rust spot then quickly wipe the cotton bud vertically downwards to streak the rust stain. Whilst the cotton bud is still damp, consider rubbing it around other areas to indicate slight wear and general dirtiness. Do not put too much rust on the model to start with, do a bit then study the effect before adding to it. Remember rust spots vary in size and are usually found on wearing surfaces such as steel gangways, the hull where the anchor hits it, and so on.

I created really deep rust patches in the paper plates by using a scalpel to tear away a small ragged piece of paper, then 'rust' it with the pen. All rust marks must be allowed to dry thoroughly before receiving a final coat of varnish.

The original wooden mast broke while the model was being loaded

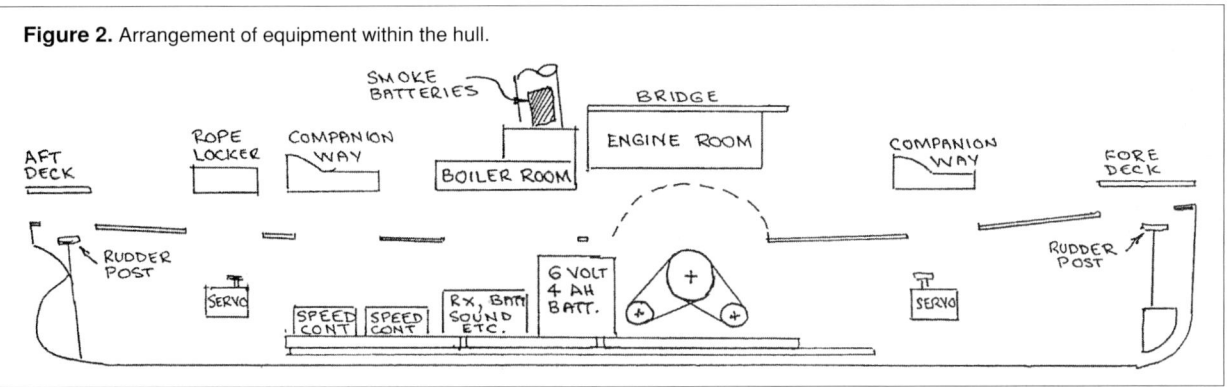

Figure 2. Arrangement of equipment within the hull.

Port paddle box showing rust marks.

into the car, and was replaced by one made from a brass tube and fittings, soft-soldered together. This is removable for storage and transport and will be modified to enable the navigation lights to work.

I considered building in some fore-and-aft deck hawsers, attached to substantial parts of the hull. These would be coiled on deck whilst *Fredrina* was underway, and used as lifting straps for launching and retrieval. This proved too difficult and I now use two straps attached to weighted wood laths/dowels to slide under the hull at bow and stern.

I made a shallow wooden box (dry dock) to facilitate *Fredrina*'s

storage, protection and transport. I intend to make one end removable so that the box can go into the hatchback with the back end tilted up so *Fredrina* can slide into the box. Together the tug and the box are a bit cumbersome and heavy for lifting in and out of the car.

I plan to fit working navigation

Port paddle box detail.

Photographs by the author.

and interior lights which are partly wired. I also have an electronic steam whistle simulator and an electronic steam engine noise simulator linked to the speed controller output. The latter is not very effective at the moment due to the amount of noise made by the gear boxes.

Initially I attempted to operate the tug using one R/C channel for each drive motor, and individual channels for each rudder. The hand/eye co-ordination proved to be a nerve-shredding, difficult task. It was during this phase that I hoisted a 'D – Delta' signal flag which means, 'Keep clear of me – I am manoeuvring with difficulty'. The next stage was to connect electrically the two rudders on to one control stick. The final simplification phase will be to fit an elec-

tronic mixer, which rationalises speed and direction control to one stick operation.

The three pole motors tend to be a bit 'notchy' at slow speed and the epicyclical gearboxes are noisy. I intend to fit 5-pole motors and modified toothed belt drives of suitable ratio during *Fredrina*'s first refit.

I suspect that the diameter of the paddle wheels is too near the internal diameter of the boxes. This may result in a build up of water in the box in operation which would reduce the efficiency. I may have to remove peripheral strips from the paddle floats.

The main problem I experienced was the difficulty of installing some of the components due to space and inaccessibility. This was due mainly

to my lack of experience in planning the order of the work.

One important lesson that I learned was the absolute necessity, before starting on any building work, to research and plan very thoroughly details, materials and construction. This should be accompanied by making copious notes and dimensioned sketches.

References

Famous Paddle Steamers by F C Hambelton, MAP 1948, Argus Press, 1971.

Model Shipwright: 41. HMS *Forceful*; 45, page 10, steering problems; 45, 46: *Eppleton Hall*; 53. Tramp Steamer *Chelford*; 90. *Viribus Unitis* and *Texas* for steel plating; 97. riveting for model shipwrights. ❏

MODELLER'S Draught

A Fair Isle Class 'Sputnik' Trawler

by J Pottinger

The shipyard at Berwick operated under a number of owners from its formation in 1950, although vessels had been built there since early times.

The well-known boat builders William Weatherhead took a lease on land at the Quayside and laid down the keel of the first boat in October 1950. This family of boat builders had operated yards in Scotland at Eyemouth, Port Seton and Cockenzie, and expanded to take over the family yard at Eyemouth in 1946.

Here they built a wide variety of wooden craft for the Admiralty during the Second World War, when links had been established with Fairmile Marine. This company had produced a number of fast motor vessels such as the Fairmile B and D types for the Royal Navy.

During this period they also produced various fittings and sub-assemblies, which were sent to yards around the country, such as that at Cockenzie, for final assembly. It was with their urging that Weatherhead were asked to consider building in steel, but at that time neither the Eyemouth or Cockenzie yards had the space, machinery or skills to do so. It was for this purpose that the Berwick yard was established.

It was when Weatherhead had financial problems after building seven barges and two small tugs that Fairmile Construction Ltd took over the running of the Berwick yard in 1953, and did so until 1972, the period between 1957 and 1961 being the most productive.

Following the opening up of fishing grounds after the end of the Second World War, government grants and loans became available to encourage and stimulate demand to rebuild the fishing fleet, which had been run down or requisitioned by the Admiralty during the war, and was in poor shape when peace came.

The Fairmile Company, recognising this need, made a study of the

Coral Isle SN22 (Ship No. 367) completed in 1956, on trials when new.

likely requirements for an economic size of vessel and of a type versatile enough to be adopted for drift net, long lining, seine netting, or trawling. At that time a comparable vessel was a trawler of around 100ft manned by a larger crew.

This provided the stimulus for the introduction of the Fair Isle class of steel trawlers, designed by the French naval architect M E R Gueroult, specifically to meet the above requirements. The first one to be completed was the *Coral Isle* SN22, which was built in 1956 under supervision by Burness, Kendall and Partners for the North Shields merchants J Rutherford, but intended to operate from Aberdeen.

The design featured a high flaring, raked bow and a rounded cruiser stern, with relatively fine underwater lines to give economy under power. Operating experience by well-known owners testified to their seaworthi-

Fern BF205 (Ship No. 484) completed in 1958 as *Summer Isle* LH69, shown new after whaleback. The wheelhouse and masts have been fitted, and rigged for trawling.

ness. It was shortly after their introduction that they were given the nickname 'Sputniks' by Aberdeen trawlermen, after the Russian manned satellite of that time.

This first boat was fitted out for seine netting, with a Sutherland four-speed winch driven by a belt

from a pulley on the forward end of a long shaft which was coupled to the forward end of the main engine. An Elliot and Garood 'Beccles' warp coiler was sited aft of the winch, and driven by a chain drive from the winch.

The hull was subdivided from for-

Another view of *Fern* with a three-quarter-length shelter deck added.

ward thus: chain locker, ballast tank with store above, insulated fish hold, engine room, aft cabin. Accommodation in the cabin, heated by a small stove, was provided for eight men, with an additional separate single cabin for the skipper. Access to the cabin was by a companionway at the aft end of the deckhouse. The galley and messroom was located in the deckhouse aft of the wheelhouse, and was fitted with an oil-burning cooking range.

The hull was of welded construction, but with double riveted sheerstrake. Oddly, the freeing ports, which were much enlarged later, cut into this strake. The shell plating was ⁵⁄₁₆in thick, riveted to the frames, which were formed from 2½in x 2½in x ⅜in angle bars. The deck plating was ¼in thick.

Specification

Length overall: 73ft 0in.
Length bp: 64ft 0in.
Beam: 19ft 0in.
Depth: 10ft 9in.
Draught aft: 8ft 9in.
Displacement: 136.73 tons.
Gross tonnage: 71.04 tons.
Engine: Gardner 8L3; 152 bhp.
Speed on trial: 9.4 knots.
Static pull: 2.15 tons at 680 rpm.

It may be of interest to note that an example of a modern twin-rig trawler of today having the same overall length has a beam of 25.2ft and a draught of 15.7ft and a gross tonnage of 201 tons, an indication of the far greater displacement and volume.

The immediate success of this design is attested to the fact that the yard was turning out boats at a rate of about five a year, and no less than twenty-three in all were completed to the same basic design. Some have operated as trawlers, seine netters and scallopers. The last of the 73ft fishing boats was completed at the beginning of 1962.

In 2006 there were two still fishing and two operating as pleasure vessels within a year of their half-century.

The withdrawal of the various grant and loan schemes resulted in the yard having to look for other types of orders to survive, and among the variety of craft constructed were seven luxury yachts, built between 1962 and 1966, based on the design of the Fair Isle hull but

Karen A416 (Ship No. 528) completed 1960, seen leaving Aberdeen as rigged for trawling with open deck and lack of any protective whaleback. Note the trawl gallows and trawl winch. The Gilson derrick has now been stepped on top of the deckhouse. Later re-registered as PZ193; sold and renamed *Our Joanne* GY7; later re-registered as FD50.

longer, with an additional few frames in the middle.

Sadly the first boat of the series, the *Coral Isle*, disappeared on the Ling Bank fishing grounds during the night of 13 December 1969 with the loss of her six crew members.

The ship

The plan shows the trawler rigged as a seine netter, which ideally would have a warp coiler mounted aft of the seine net winch, and chain driven from the winch. This item is fairly complex in design, and not having sufficient detail date to work up a reasonable drawing, I have purposely omitted it.

In fact, in the early days of seine netting the coiling of the warps was all done by hand, and laid in coils along the side decks. After the advent of the coiler, the warps were still laid down as previously. A later

Fran WK493, ex-*Bon Accord* A493 (Ship No. 546) completed 1960, and seen here on the pontoon at Aberdeen as a trawler, also as PD244.

innovation was the provision of warp bins, being cylindrical tubes projecting down into the hull, with the top flush with the deck, allowing the warps to be coiled and stowed in the bins directly off the coiler.

The advent of large rope reels, which could reel on the whole length

of the warps directly from the winch, was the final development.

Note that the vertical roller shown mounted on the starboard side of the wheelhouse should be positioned slightly further down to ensure a clear lead of the warp from the winch to the roller on the bulwark on the starboard quarter.

Denarius BF804, ex-*Shamal* BF16, ex-*Craigielea* A320 (Ship No. 514), completed in 1958. Shown as a twin-rig trawler. Also operated as *Harvester II* AH108, *Onam* BF433 and *Jaseline* INS248.

This shows *Fran* at a later date under tow and now as a scalloper.

The illustrations show some of the different rigs and conversions, which were carried out on these boats at various stages of their career, often completely transforming the appearance from the original. It is noticeable that the added weight of trawl winches, gallows and shelter decks, etc., has lessened the freeboard from that as designed and as shown in the trials view of the *Coral Isle*.

Model notes

To fit within the required page format I have had to show only a half deck plan, but the port half mirrors that shown except for the cod end derrick and warp roller, which are on the starboard side of the wheelhouse side only. The dead-lights shown on the starboard side are repeated on the port side, with an additional port side deadlight shown dotted.

The winch itself is driven by a geared shaft drive taken directly off a jockey pulley mounted on deck, which in turn is driven by a belt extending up from a pulley on the forward end of a long shaft which runs under the fish hold floor-boards, and is coupled via 2:1 step down gearing power take-off from the forward end of the crankshaft.

When rigged for trawling a trawl winch would be installed in front of the wheelhouse, with gallows located fore and aft just inside the bulwarks, and with pedestal-mounted rollers to guide the warps from the foot blocks on the gallows to the winch.

Zephyrus BCK269, ex-*Mistletoe* FR304, ex-*Confederate* (Ship No. 549) completed 1960.

Mary Croan LH225 (Ship No. 485) completed 1958, seen in Loch Linnhe. Unusually she has her seine net winch and warp coiler forward of the foremast. This was due to the position of the mast as being relatively far aft, precluding the sitting of the winch aft of the mast, due to insufficient space to fleet the warps on the side decks, as a result of the layout of the fish ponds amidships. In this position there was enough room to haul the warps 'downhill' aft off the coiler along the deck. Also named *Ocean Bounty* BF7.

Photographs from the author's collection.

At 1:25 scale these plans will give a reasonable sized model for power operation, with plenty of space for power and control mechanisms.

The whole deckhouse can be made to lift off, and further access to any equipment can be via the central hatch. The open grating over the steering quadrant can be laid on top of a solid base, which in turn can hide a hatch giving access to the steering gear.

The wooden deck is set on a steel plate base, with boundaries as shown, and with margin planks around the various deck structures. The fish pond boards on the starboard side abreast the deckhouse have a depth equal to half the height of the bulwarks. A fixed cod end derrick is positioned to bring aboard the cod

end for emptying in these enclosures. The rudder quadrant aft is connected to the steering wheel in the wheelhouse by a rod and chain system. Rods are used in the middle where the run is straight. Chain is used between the after end of the after rod and the quadrant. Similarly, chain runs from the fore end of the forward rod to the steering gypsy in the wheelhouse.

The foremast is mounted in a tabernacle. An extended bracket on the after bulkhead of the deckhouse carries the mizzen boom gooseneck fitting, and a small mizzen sail can be an optional addition if preferred.

Colour scheme

This depended on the owner's or skipper's preference, but a suggested livery is as follows:

Blue: hull above waterline, inside of bulwarks, exhaust casing, winch and belt cover, cowl at top of wheelhouse.

Red: hull underbody.

White: line at waterline, wheelhouse and casing, name and port of registration number, mast top section.

Varnished: masts below, white top section and spars.

References

Fairmile Construction Company Ltd brochure 'New Type of Fishing Boat'. Website: http://www.berwickshipyard.com/Fishing%20Vessels.html